THIRD EDITION

Dr. Temple Grandin & Kate Duffy

DEVELOPING TALENTS

Careers for Individuals with Autism

DEVELOPING TALENTS: Careers for Individuals with Autism

All marketing and publishing rights guaranteed to and reserved by:

FUTURE HORIZONS

(817) 277-0727

(817) 277-2270 (fax)

E-mail: info@fhautism.com

www.fhautism.com

ISBN: 978-1-957984-71-1

Contents

CHAPTER 3

Rules for Success on the Job
55

CHAPTER 4
Finding a Vocation You Love
79

CHAPTER 5
Searching for an Ideal Job
101

CHAPTER 6
Do What You Do Best
125

CHAPTER 7
Best Jobs for Individuals on the Autism Spectrum
139

CHAPTER 8

Entrepreneurship
209

CHAPTER 9

Advice from Those Who Have Gone Before
219

Foreword

A relatively small proportion of adults with autism achieve long-term employment appropriate to their intellectual ability and qualifications. This is a remarkable waste of potential talent. The American workforce needs the benefit of the qualities of these individuals.

Temple Grandin is a pioneer in terms of her ability to achieve highly successful employment, capitalizing on the very qualities associated with autism spectrum disorders. This book is somewhat like Temple herself: practical, knowledgeable, and positive. Together with Kate Duffy, a specialist in career planning, she has written a book that will be of great value to parents, teachers, and employment agencies, as well as adults with autism.

The book provides advice and illustrations from Temple's own experiences as well as the advice of other autistic people who have also achieved lucrative and enjoyable careers. While the benefits in income and independence from successful employment are obvious, I would add that there is another important benefit. As a clinician, I have noted that adults with autism tend to define themselves by their employment rather than their social network. In other words, their self-esteem is based on the quality of their work. Not surprisingly, therefore, one of the causes of depression in this population is a lack of successful and enjoyable employment. This book has the potential to significantly improve the quality of life of people with autism, their families, and society.

— Professor Tony Attwood

Dear Parents, Teachers and Counselors from Temple Grandin and Kate Duffy

Thank you for reading this third edition of *Developing Talents*. When we started working on the first edition in 2002, we were frustrated and concerned by the large number of people on the autism spectrum who either didn't have a job or held one that was much beneath their abilities or talents. Work is so important to the human experience in our culture, and here were great numbers of people who would never know the joy of completing a project, contributing financially to their families, or maybe even living on their own someday.

This was dismal news.

That is why we wrote the first and second editions of what has become a widely used and read resource: to help others on the spectrum learn to find jobs and careers where they could shine.

It is now February 2024 and the revised edition of *Developing Talents* is about to go to the printer. We're afraid our concern about high school and college graduates with autism not getting and keeping good jobs still rings true. This is most often due to a lack of career-relevant job experiences before they graduate.

What happened? It is not that there aren't jobs that these graduates would be good at. Many jobs would be a perfect fit for the analytical, detail-oriented, and precise talents of young people on the high-functioning end of the autism spectrum. This book lists quite a few in Chapters

6 and 7. In Denmark, Thorkil Sonne has even made a case that his 75 employees with autism have given his software testing firm a competitive advantage. Who, after all, is more passionate about detail and precision than someone on the spectrum? Sonne, the father of a child on the spectrum, purposely created Specialisterne (www. specialisterne.com) as a workplace haven of sorts for those with Asperger's, with its well-defined expectations, organized office space, and less stressful environment.

Specialisterne's clients have included corporate giants Microsoft and Oracle, and before new employees can even think about getting close to one of their software programs, they have to know what is expected of them, technically and socially. Employees have to keep their cool and work hard to have an interesting and fulfilling job. In other words, Sonne's employees have to pay attention to what the company needs and wants from them in order to be successful. Not a bad trade-off; people have been doing it for years. But there seem to be an awful lot of young people who haven't learned about that trade-off, who aren't particularly interested in what other people need or want—even employers.

Work Skills Are Different Than Academic Skills

I have spent over 50 years designing equipment for the livestock industry and have been a university professor for 34 years. I had no speech until age four, and I want to thank my mother and the many teachers and mentors who worked with me. Over the years, I have collaborated with many successful people who probably had undiagnosed autism. Grandparents frequently come up to me at conferences and tell me that they discovered they were autistic after the kids got diagnosed. They were able to keep good jobs because they learned work skills when they were young.

Work skills and academic skills are totally different. Too many autistic teens and young adults have also not learned life skills, such as shopping, budgeting, and personal hygiene. There is often a tendency for parents to overprotect and do too many tasks for their child. But it is never too late for an autistic adult to learn work skills. The first step is learning how to do a task on a schedule for somebody OUTSIDE the family. Some possible tasks could be walking the neighbor's dog or helping an elderly neighbor. I met an autistic teen who was so proud that she was the "coffee lady" at her church. She was successfully doing a task for people outside her family.

In my livestock-equipment design work, I have worked with many talented metal workers, designers, and welders. During their careers, they have invented and patented complex mechanical equipment. About 20 percent of them were either undiagnosed autistic, were dyslexic, or had ADHD. They had taken shop classes in high school, and some of them had started at entry-level jobs. They gradually worked their way up because they were skilled at many things. This way of getting a good job still works today. Recently, I talked to two people who got great jobs fixing industrial equipment. They started as laborers, and they learned to repair many types of machines on the job.

Today, there is a huge need for high-level skilled trades jobs. The good thing about these jobs is that they will not be replaced by artificial intelligence (AI). An AI program is not going to install the electrical wiring in your house or repair an elevator. Recently, I visited a program in Denver that teaches auto mechanics to young autistic adults. They have been very successful getting their trainees hired by auto dealers. They have been successful because they taught BOTH mechanical and life skills. Along with the mechanics, the students learned how to be on time and have good personal hygiene. When they get a job at an auto dealer, they also had a job coach for several months. The mechanics classes were kept small with six students.

Introduce Change Slowly

We know that people on the spectrum tend to resist change and many lack the motivation to try new things. In my own case, as a teenager I didn't want to spend the summer at my aunt's ranch out west. One of the reasons was that they had no TV at the ranch. Mother insisted that I go but told me that if I hated it, I could come home after two weeks.

I ended up staying all summer! I loved the ranch, and my favorite TV show soon became less important. In fact, staying at the ranch started my cattle chute obsession, which formed the starting point for my career. But first,

I had to move from my obsession of talking about cattle chutes to designing cattle facilities. Sometimes parents and teachers have to push an individual on the spectrum to try new things.

But expect that pushing to bear fruit slowly. My mother told me for two months that I would be spending that summer on my aunt's ranch. In a way I was prepared to go, even though I didn't like the idea. Here are some other ways for young people on the spectrum to prepare for a life of their own:

1. Go slowly, but go in the direction that interests you by holding down a job or an internship, preferably in a field in which you're interested in working. The three Aspies who tell their stories in Chapter 9 all had jobs when they were in high school. They gained work experience by delivering newspapers, mowing lawns, selling greeting cards, and working in a store and on a farm.

2. Study other people's needs as a way to learn about the world. In high school and college, I had a sign-painting business, and even though I couldn't have cared less about beauty salons, I still had to pay attention to what the owner wanted on her sign. I also built sets for the high school plays, and even though I really wanted to build cow chutes or barns, I couldn't. That's not what the director needed.

3. In college, take a lighter load of classes and continue to get work experience. At work you have to learn

how to get along with others and keep your cool when you feel like blowing your stack. If you make jokes about the fat lady in the elevator, you'll be fired. Or if you have a meltdown because the break room offered the wrong kind of cookies that day, you'll also be fired. Both of these, unfortunately, are true stories.

4. Introduce change slowly in your life. Remember that the executive function part of the autistic brain doesn't work so well, so expect to feel confused some of the time. It is best to avoid multitasking, and if you have trouble organizing your day, make a written schedule of your activities.

5. Lighten up. Expect that you'll be upset and perturbed part of the day and design your schedule around those times. Do more complex tasks at times of the day when you feel the most energetic. Laugh deeply and often and join the world as much as you can. After all, you are a member of the human race, and this is your home.

Young people on the autism spectrum have talents and have a lot to contribute to the world. In this third edition of *Developing Talents*, we have added a chapter (Chapter 8) on a growing area of the U.S. economy: entrepreneurship. Many of the unique characteristics of individuals on the autism spectrum lend themselves well to taking advantage of, and thriving on, the wide-open possibilities of this field.

During my 35-year career in the livestock industry, I have worked with successful colleagues who are on the Asperger/autism spectrum. These include designers, computer programmers, engineers, statisticians, building contractors, radio and print journalists, animal trainers, and professors. Most of these people were never diagnosed. To inspire young people on the spectrum to work hard and get into good careers, we have added a new chapter (Chapter 9), in which three successful autistic people offer advice.

In addition, Chapter 4 presents information about vocational rehabilitation programs that provide job training and placement for people with disabilities as well as information about Social Security Administration programs that provide vocational assistance. Chapter 4 also includes a profile of a mother of a child on the spectrum who has helped her son achieve independence through a blend of persistence, creativity, and ongoing advocacy. Finally, we have listed new jobs that are particularly well-suited for those on the spectrum.

The world is an interesting place, and individuals on the autism spectrum miss out on a lot if they ignore it. They will miss out even more if they can't figure out their fellow human beings' needs. Please help them pay attention; they'll have a much better life as a result.

Tips for Keeping Jobs

For many years, I have observed certain patterns occurring over time that have caused a loss of jobs. Some simple accommodations would prevent many jobs from being lost:

- Explaining a task with long strings of verbal instruction does not work. This is due to poor working memory. Any task that requires a sequence of steps should be presented in a written "pilot's checklist" format. The steps for performing the task should be presented on a list of bullet points. There was a sad case of an electrician apprentice who lost his job because he installed the wrong switches and light fixture. He was not able to remember a long list of verbal instructions. He would probably still have his job if he had been given a written list.
- Avoid jobs with rapid multitasking such as a busy food takeout window.
- There are some accommodations that will have to be made for sensory issues. There is a whole chapter in the book about this.
- Vague instructions from the boss do not work. Telling an employee that they are not a team player is too vague. The autistic employee needs to be taken to a private office and directly instructed on how to behave. For example, calling Jim a jerk at the project meeting was not acceptable and they will have to apologize.

- A danger area for many autistic employees is when they get a new boss. I almost lost an early job writing for a livestock magazine when I got a new boss. I was able to save my job by showing the new boss a portfolio of my articles. He thought I was weird, but he formed a different opinion after he saw some of my good work. I learned to sell my skills to people by showing a portfolio of my work.

— Temple Grandin

Hello, readers.

Thank you for joining us for this third edition of *Developing Talents*. It's been fifteen years since we released the last edition, and in that time there have been some positive changes in the employment landscape for individuals on the autism spectrum. Five worth paying attention to are below:

- *A shift in how government agencies view employment for people with disabilities*—Nationwide, more states are involved in the Employment First initiative, a national movement to ensure people with disabilities, no matter how severe, are able to participate in "competitive integrated employment" and community life. Simply put, employment in the community is a primary goal and is to be supported by the state agencies providing vocational services to people with disabilities.
- *Increased access to inclusive academic/vocational education after high school*—More than 300 universities and colleges now offer inclusive higher-education programs to students with intellectual and developmental disabilities (IDD), including autism. These programs provide students with academic, vocational, and independent living experiences that help students work towards their personal and vocational goals. Each institution structures its program differently, but all have the mission of

helping their students transition more seamlessly to the workforce and their community. The Institute for Community Inclusion, UMass Boston provides technical assistance, evaluation, and research services to inclusive education programs through its national center, Think College, where you can find a listing of colleges and universities offering inclusive education.

- *Corporations partnering with disability-inclusion experts*—More corporations are diversifying their workforce by partnering with disability-inclusion experts such as James Emmett and Company to create systems for recruiting, hiring, training, and retaining employees with autism and other disabilities. Emmett, who has a disability and three daughters with disabilities, has worked closely with companies such as Walgreens, Office Max/Depot, PepsiCo, and others to increase their capacity for hiring employees with disabilities.

- *Job and career mapping tools for all*—Thanks to organizations such as the DeBruce Foundation, students and community members, with and without disabilities, are discovering and matching their talents, interests, and skills to jobs where they can shine. DeBruce's Agile Work Profiler is free and aims to help individuals of all ages learn how their strengths can add value to the workforce, even in entry-level jobs. The Foundation's goal is to increase career pathways and job seekers' ability to take more control of their economic lives. DeBruce partners with school districts, higher education institutions, community organizations, government agencies and more to train their teachers and staff to use the Agile Work Profiler with students and clients they serve.

- *Planning and organizing tools to help navigate systems*—Finally, individuals with disabilities, parents, special education teachers, disability service coordinators, counselors and others across the country have used the Charting the LifeCourse planning tools to organize their vision and goals as well as navigate and advocate for supports. LifeCourse is a powerful planning tool used by many agencies and families to ensure their clients or family members live a life that is important to them.

Given these positives, why then is the employment rate still so low for people with disabilities, 21.3 percent in 2022, including autism (U.S. Bureau of Labor Statistics)? The answer is pretty straightforward: Underfunded and often understaffed, the employment system for people with disabilities is broken, creating a kind of limbo for adults with autism and their families.

Mine has been one of those families for the past several years, as my older son has gone through severe, debilitating bouts of anxiety, not uncommon for adults with autism. Our family has always believed that "everyone works," no matter the disability or challenge. My son has worked off and on since he was 17, needing few supports, especially in those jobs that were a good fit for his talents and interests.

As he has aged, though, his anxieties have grown, and his autistic obsessions intensified. Finding and keeping a job has proven to be difficult. Last year, an employment specialist referred him away from Vocational Rehabilitation services to the more intensive supports of a state Medicaid Home and Community Based Services (HCBS) employment services program. It took a year to get through the paperwork and "wait list," an eternity for my son and the rest of us.

My son is not alone in needing this extra help, according to Drexel University autism researchers Anne Roux and Lindsay Shea. Their September 2023 opinion piece in *Scientific American* estimates "that half of autistic individuals (adults) in the U.S., or about 2.7 million people, require some services to find and keep a job. Poverty rates are higher than average among families with autistic individuals, so many autistic people must rely on public employment services. Unfortunately, most of these individuals will never receive them."

This is a terrible loss. Lives on hold, talents wasted, opportunities missed. We spend most of our lives as adults, Roux and Shea argue, so why not mandate developmental-disability services throughout adulthood and invest more in in-home and community-based care? The numbers they cite make their case:

- Only 1.1 percent of adults with autism who likely needed job supports received public employment services in 2016 through Medicaid or state vocational rehabilitation programs
- Forty-two percent of autistic youth don't have jobs in their early 20s
- Fewer than 1 in 5 adults with autism who receive public employment services have a paid job in the community

What can change this dismal picture is for those of us in the autism community, self-advocates, and supporters alike, to join together to lobby for increased funding and more accountability on how those dollars serve our communities. Families have a long history of organizing to create, and lobby for, services for their children with disabilities. The National Alliance for the Mentally Ill (NAMI), Autism Delaware Adult Services, The Mission Project, The Arc Jacksonville Village, and Casa Familia are several examples.

You'll find that much of our career advice in this third edition has stayed the same over the years. We still advocate for youth and adults with autism to select jobs reflecting their interests and talents. Everybody does

That is partly true because autism brains tend to be specialized, good at some things and not so good at others. We want readers on the spectrum to pay close attention to how they take in and process information, their thinking styles, so to speak. In general, there are three different specialized brains: visual, or thinking in pictures; music, higher math or pattern thinking; and verbal lists and language translator. Once again, we have a list of jobs that people with these different brain or processing styles would do well at.

— **Kate Duffy**

Sources

Bureau of Labor Statistics, U.S. Department of Labor, *The Economics Daily*, Employment–population ratio for people with a disability increases to 21.3 percent in 2022 at https://www.bls.gov/opub/ted/2023/employment-population-ratio-for-people-with-a-disability-increases-to-21-3-percent-in-2022.htm (visited December 25, 2023).

Roux, Anne, and Lindsay Shea. "A Broken Employment System Leaves Autistic Adults Stranded." *Scientific American*: Sept 13, 2023. www.scientificamerican.com accessed 12.25.2023.

Introduction
Some of the Most Brilliant Minds Are Autistic

Whenever I attend autism conferences, I am struck by how many people on the fully verbal end of the autism spectrum are either unemployed or underemployed. This really bothers me because working is such an important part of my life. Without work, no matter how big or small the job, life would become small and unsatisfying for me. With work, we discover we can give back to our family and community that have given so much to us.

Yet, I realize that the idea that people with autism spectrum disorders can work in a meaningful job sounds unrealistic to many. But as someone with autism who has run a freelance livestock equipment design business and held down a part-time college professor job for more than three decades, I know it can be done, and, I believe, should be done. For one, we do not want our autism to be the whole of our lives. That is neither healthy nor wise. I think that people who are able should get out in the community and get jobs.

Just as important, society loses out if individuals with autism spectrum disorders are not involved in the world of work or make other kinds of contributions to society.

Some of our world's finest minds, inventions, art, and ideas belong to people with autistic traits (Fitzgerald & O'Brien, 2007). Albert Einstein and Vincent Van Gogh, for example, both had developmental abnormalities during early childhood, as explored in my earlier book *Thinking in Pictures* (2006). In my new book *Visual Thinking: The Hidden Gifts of People Who Think in Pictures, Patterns, and Abstractions*, I discuss individuals who have more recently been identified as either autistic or having autistic traits. Some of them are Elon Musk, Greta Thurnberg, Steve Jobs, and Mark Zuckerberg. There is additional information about Elon Musk in Vance (2015) and Isaacson (2023).

Over the years, the criteria for diagnosing autism have changed. In the 1980's, a child had to have BOTH speech delay and symptoms such as, being society isolated and repetitive behavior, to be diagnosed with autism. In 1994, Asperger's Syndrome was added to the *Diagnostic and Statistical Manual* that was published by the American Psychiatric Association. It is basically socially awkward with no obvious speech delay. In 2013 (DSM-5, 2022) the Asperger diagnosis was removed and the individuals with no speech delay were merged with the individuals with either speech delay or no speech. This created a huge autism spectrum that ranged from non-speaking individuals with intellectual disability, to Einsteins. These individuals are some non-speaking individuals who have learned to type independently and have normal intelligence.

These kids are often the really bright science "nerds." Einstein, for one, did not associate with his peers at school. He had tremendous single-mindedness in solving problems—but only those that interested him!

Oddly enough, it may have been that very social backwardness that led Einstein to develop his theory of relativity. After all, how many "normal" adults spend a lot of time thinking about the problems of space and time? As an adult, Einstein continued to demonstrate the traits of someone with mild autism. He cared little for social niceties, wore disheveled clothes, and kept his hair long and unruly. His students and colleagues reported that his lectures were scattered and sometimes incomprehensible. Often he would stop in the middle of writing a theorem on the board, seem to go into a trance, and then emerge from it a few minutes later only to write a new hypothesis (Clark, 1971; Fitzgerald & O'Brien, 2007).

Similarly, biographers describe artist Vincent Van Gogh as an odd, aloof child who threw many tantrums and preferred spending time alone. He was ill-groomed and blunt and spoke with tension and a nervous rasp in his voice, quite common for adults with autistic tendencies. He was also terribly self-absorbed when he spoke with others and cared little about his listeners' interest or comfort, according to Grant (1968).

Often, individuals on the autism spectrum do not do well in school. I had a horrible time graduating from high school myself. Many renowned scientists, artists, and writers also had difficulties in school. For example, Gregor Mendel, the father of modern genetics, could not pass the exam to get a high school teaching license. He conducted his experiments in the corner of a monastery garden with pea plants. When he presented the results of his experiments at his thesis defense, he failed to get his degree.

Nobody paid any attention to his ideas, but thankfully 120 copies of his paper survived and were recognized as the works of genius that they are after his death. Even though sometimes subject to debate, today, Mendel's principles are taught in every high school science class (Fitzgerald & O'Brien, 2007; Kevin, 1967).

Philosopher Ludwig Wittgenstein probably had autism, suggests neurologist Oliver Sacks (1995). He did not talk until he was four years old and was considered a dullard with no talent. Other members of his family presumably suffered from depression, quite common among individuals with autism spectrum disorders. Indeed, both of his brothers committed suicide. Among his talents, Wittgenstein had strong mechanical abilities, building a sewing machine at the age of ten. He used formal language, even with his peers, who teased him about his odd speech and mannerisms. We now know that overly formal speech is common in individuals on the autism spectrum.

As these examples illustrate, if we leave out certain people from society's work, we all lose out. Other famous people who were probably on the autism spectrum include Thomas Jefferson, Carl Sagan, and Amadeus Mozart (Ledgin, 2001).

For those on the autism spectrum, finding a satisfying job also provides social opportunities through shared interests. Some of the most satisfying experiences in my life have been interacting with engineers and the people I worked with to build the facilities I had designed. It was one "techie" communicating with another "techie."

Productive Work Makes Life Satisfying

Work is more than just a livelihood or paycheck; it is the key to a satisfying and productive life. For many on the autism spectrum, it is the glue that keeps our lives together in an otherwise frustrating and sometimes confusing world. Certainly, my life would not be worth living if I did not have intellectually satisfying work.

On a related note, I remember reading a few years ago about free Linux software. People in the business world had difficulty comprehending why the programmers gave their work away. But it's not a mystery to me why they would download their programs, their "ideas," into the great and evolving computer operating system.

How wonderful to know your thoughts and work live on as part of the "genetic code" of a computer program. The Linux people are putting themselves into the program, contributing their "intellectual DNA" to the forever cyberspace. As the program evolves, the code they wrote will remain buried deep within it, becoming part of the great evolution of computer science. These programmers contribute to this effort because it makes their lives more meaningful.

I realize that many people on the autism spectrum, especially those with more severe autism, will not go to college, or hold down a job that requires a higher education degree. Many jobs do not require a four-year college degree, but the best-paying jobs do require some formal education or training after high school. The most important thing jobs require is for the job holder to be willing to work and have a good attitude at work. In other words, be willing to learn new skills, get along with coworkers, and do the best job you can. Many people with autism do well in college, for example, but have problems keeping a job upon graduation. This book will provide information that will help you develop your talents and get and keep a good job.

Even people on the non-speaking end of the autism spectrum can work if they are coached along the way and eased into the workplace. In a way, I am my work, which provides a much-needed framework for my life. Because of my work as a livestock facilities designer and an animal science professor, I have regular and frequent contact with other people. We discuss projects, plan programs, and brainstorm ideas. Yet, I spend most of my weekend time alone, drawing and reading. If it weren't for my job, I'm afraid I would spend even more of my time secluded, isolated from the world I now navigate with some ease. This ease was hard-won and only came because of the many interventions and support I received over the years. These form the basis for the ideas and suggestions in this book.

As I look back, my mother made sure I received speech therapy, a good preschool education, and a lot of help at home with social skills and manners at an early age. I was not motivated to study in high school because the sub-jects seemed boring to me. Biology class and working on construction projects were my main interest. Luckily, my high school science teacher used my interests to motivate me to study. We did interesting science projects, and in the process I realized I had to study "the boring stuff" to reach my goal of becoming a scientist.

Mentors were another important influence in my life and career. My high school science teacher mentored me, even into college, and several employers mentored me at my first jobs.

When my anxieties grew overwhelming, I turned to medication that helped me stay on an even keel. I realize that medication is not the answer for everyone. Yet, all of the above—and more—have allowed me to continue the work I love.

As long as the livestock industry continues to use the handling facilities and equipment I have designed for the past 50 years, my thoughts live and my life has meaning. If my efforts to improve the treatment of cattle and pigs make real improvement in the world, my life is meaningful.

This book was born out of my frustration and fear that many on the autism spectrum were missing out on the very important experience of work. I feared they would never know the satisfaction of contributing to their fami-lies and their communities, of being independent and economically self-sufficient.

To build success, parents should help their children develop their natural talents. Often, these talents are the first steps toward a paying job later on. Drawing, writing, building models, programming computers or landscaping yards—all of these can grow into paying jobs. Talent speaks for itself and can sell itself, if given a chance and a decent portfolio.

Parents must also help young people learn the skills needed to find and keep a job. These skills are first learned at home. In hindsight, I was lucky to be a child of the 1950s. The more structured lifestyle that was prevalent then was very helpful to me. For example, meals with the entire family provided opportunities to learn social skills. Other helpful activities included playing lots of board games and card games where, among other things, I learned to take turns. I was expected to sit still through dinner, to be polite to others, to do my chores, and to get along with my siblings. As I grew older, I was expected to work. At age 13, I held down my first job, working two afternoons a week as a seamstress' assistant. Later I worked on my aunt's ranch, at a school for children with autism and other conditions, and at a research lab when I was a college student. Although I wasn't crazy about all of my jobs all of the time, they forced me to become more responsible.

Although my parents provided plenty of assistance for me, they also had high expectations. It is those expectations that have helped me navigate the world. For youths on the autism spectrum, this is especially important because they will have to work harder to prove themselves in our fast- paced, competitive global economy. The good news is that with the tremendous labor shortage facing the United States when the baby boomers retire in the next five to ten years, employers will look more to those of us with disabilities to fill jobs for which we once would not have been considered.

Finally, young people need a mentor to give them guidance and valuable experience. Mentors introduce their protégées to the world, helping them find ways to navigate the sometimes confusing byways that life presents. After the initial introduction, they also help their protégées stay on track and develop their talents by serving as the sounding board for ideas, plans, and dreams.

This book is designed to take readers—those on the autism spectrum and their family members, teachers, counselors, and other adults who make a difference in young lives—through the career-planning process. It includes information on discovering and growing the talents and interests that might lead to satisfying work as well as a career-planning and job-search process. These are ideas that have helped me succeed:

Chapter 1, "Autism Spectrum Disorders and Their Effect in the Workplace," includes a discussion of the characteristics of autism spectrum disorders (ASD) as they relate to the workplace.

Chapter 2, "Easing into the Workplace," focuses on:
- Sensory issues, anger management, medications
- Advice on developing and using social skills on the job

- Information about organizational skills to help you thrive on the job

Chapter 3, "Rules for Success on the Job," describes the strategies and skills you need to acquire to help make your work life more successful and fulfilling.

Chapter 4, "Finding a Vocation You Love," is a young people's guide to finding a vocation that will not only feed their souls but also help put food on the table. This includes a section on taking advantage of the services offered by Vocational Rehabilitation.

In Chapter 5, "Searching for an Ideal Job," you'll find information about the job search process.

Chapter 6, "Do What You Do Best," lists jobs that are particularly appropriate for the different ways of thinking that characterize those of us on the autism spectrum:
- Visual thinkers
- Music/math brains
- Nonvisual thinkers with verbal brains

Chapter 7, "Best Jobs for Individuals on the Autism Spectrum," consists of profiles of careers and jobs suited for individuals on the autism spectrum. An aircraft mechanic, computer programmer, industrial equipment specialist, librarian, and others tell their own stories on how they got into their successful careers.

Chapter 8, "Entrepreneurship," explores this burgeoning area with a special focus on the pros and cons for individuals on the autism spectrum. Great advice is offered by the Abilities Fund, a national community development organization designed to advance entrepreneurial opportunities for Americans with disabilities.

Chapter 9, "Advice from Those Who Have Gone Before: Autistic Individuals Tell Their Stories," consists of the stories of three individuals on the autism spectrum who have been successful in their careers. The chapter gives first-hand insights into the different paths and routes people take in discovering the work that fits them.

Finally, the book concludes with an appendix that consists of:

- References and resources
- Information on employees' legal rights in the workplace under the Americans with Disabilities Act
- A brief discussion on self-disclosure in the workplace
- Job search tips

I hope you will find this information useful as you begin your job search or business exploration. Good luck to you and happy job hunting.

—Temple Grandin

CHAPTER 1

Autism Spectrum Disorders and Their Effect in the Workplace

A s mentioned earlier, I had my first paying job during the summer when I was 13 years old. It was my mother's idea. I was moping around the house a lot, so she sent me to work two afternoons a week for her friend, a seamstress, who needed an extra set of hands in her business.

It was a perfect fit, for I loved to sew and loved to create the designs I saw in my head. I had been sewing for several years and was put to work doing the basics, ripping out seams and hemming pants. Going to work was the best thing for me; I had less time to mope and more time to learn how to negotiate the outside world.

That early work experience was exactly what I needed, and, frankly, what all of us on the autism spectrum need in order to achieve balance and success in our lives. Work is such a big part of the human experience that it's important for all to hold a job, no matter how big or small. We learn so much from working that it would be a shame to miss out on those experiences. For example, working teaches us how to get along with other people who are not part of our family; it helps us to become independent in our adult years; and it can give great satisfaction to know we are contributing to our own, as well as our family's well-being.

My job with the seamstress helped me become more independent and learn how to relate to others outside my small world of family and school. But sending me to work at age 13 was just one of a long list of interventions my mother created for me, starting with preschool and speech therapy.

Independence did not come easy, but I learned it because my family expected me to. The first two chapters of this book take a hard look at the challenges those with autism spectrum disorders (ASD) may face in the workplace and some tried-and-true interventions and solutions. These interventions can free us up so we can develop our talents and live fuller, more gratifying lives. It is by developing our talents that we can step more easily into the work world and find jobs that are a good fit for us. Sewing, for me, was one of those talents, and I'm forever thankful to my mother's friend for taking me on as a helper. That job helped me learn work skills.

At the same time, my family also enrolled me in a boarding school that had a farm, which nurtured my love of animals. I spent much of my teen years showing horses at 4-H fairs. Sewing and animal care may sound like an odd combination of hobbies, but I loved them both, and they led me to my present occupation as an animal scientist. In high school, I used my sewing skills to make fancy decorated halters and bridles for the horses.

During my five years at boarding school, I also worked on shingling the barn roof and building a new addition on the house. I loved construction work. Both sewing and construction work require visual thinking skills and putting things together. For the first four years, I seldom studied until I was motivated by Mr. Carlock, the science teacher, who, as mentioned, became one of my most important mentors.

My interest in livestock facilities began after I spent a summer on my aunt Brecheen's ranch in Arizona. I grew fixated on the equipment used to hold the cattle while they received injections or brandings. That fixation led me to into a career that I still care very much about, some 40 years later.

I do not mean to make my entry into the work world sound easy. It has not been. What I have noticed about those on the autism spectrum who successfully hold down jobs is that we share three characteristics:

1. Somebody helped us develop our birthright talents.
2. We had mentors during our teen and later years who helped us develop both social and job-related professional skills.
3. Where appropriate, we took medication or other treatments, including exercise, special diets or nutritional supplements, to help us manage our sensory

problems and accompanying depression and anxiety. (I realize not everyone benefits from medication, but it is an option that should not be ruled out.)

I deeply appreciate my family's hard work in raising me with a strong work ethic, but one thing is clear: all the work ethic in the world won't help me hold down a job if I can't manage my sensory system and other challenges the autism spectrum presents.

In the following, we will take a brief look at the causes and characteristics of ASD. Throughout this book, we are aiming it at fully verbal individuals. This discussion of causes and characteristics is by no means exhaustive or comprehensive as many other books and scientific reports have addressed these topics in great detail. Also, for our purposes, the main focus is on those aspects of autism spectrum disorders that have the greatest bearing on entering and surviving in the workplace.

Autism: Definition and Causes

Autism is a condition that affects every family member of the person on the autism spectrum. The rigors of raising a child on the autism spectrum to a fulfilling adulthood are daunting for a very good reason: autism affects every aspect of life.

The Autism Society of America defines autism as a complex developmental disability that typically appears during the first three years of life. The autism continuum ranges from a brilliant scientist to a nonverbal individual who will always have to live under supervised conditions. Some non-verbal people will be capable of doing a job and others simply are not. The result of a neurological disorder that affects the functioning of the brain, autism primarily impacts the normal development of the brain in the areas of social interaction and communication skills. Therefore, children and adults with autism typically have difficulties in verbal and nonverbal communication, social interactions, and leisure or play activities (www.autism-society.org).

Research indicates that the brains of people with autism have abnormal underdevelopment in the limbic system that is the center of emotions (Bauman & Kemper, 1994). In the frontal cortex, there is uncontrolled over-growth of neurons (Courchesne et al., 2001). Those brain abnormalities cause many of the autistic symptoms. The severity of the autism is related to the amount of abnormal development. The rear half of the cortex where memories are stored is relatively normal. Lucina Q. Uddin at the Department of Psychiatry, University of California states that some individuals with autism "have unique skills that potentially enable them to make significant contributions to the work force.(Uddin, 2022).

Research indicates that some individuals on the spectrum may have extra brain circuits (Cassanova et al., 2006; Courchesne & Pierce, 2005). These circuits may explain special abilities in art or math. Brain scans done on me by Nancy Minshew and her colleagues at the University of

Pittsburgh showed that I have a gigantic "Internet cable" that extends deep into my visual cortex. This may explain my visualization skills.

In 2023 the Centers for Disease Control and Prevention reported that 1 in 36 children in America today have an autism spectrum disorder. Worldwide, autism appears at the same rate as in the United States, with four times as many boys suffering from it as girls. And as in the United States, autism affects people of all races, incomes, ethnic groups and religions. The children with speech delay usually get diagnosed at an early age but the older children and adults may get diagnosed later due to being very socially awkward and not having friends.

Because autism is a "spectrum disorder," the symptoms appear in a wide variety of combinations, from mild to severe. The Autism Society of America (www.autism-society.org) notes that people on the autism spectrum may act very differently from each other, even if they have the same diagnosis. For example, some are nonverbal while others are capable of communicating successfully. Some on the spectrum are sensitive to smells while others are sensitive to touch, and so on.

Researchers are still not certain what causes autism, but they do know that it is a genetic disorder involving many interacting factors. Some researchers are studying possible links between heredity, genetics, and certain medical problems such as Fragile X Syndrome. Others are investigating a possible relationship between a cluster of unstable genes that may affect brain development and cause autism. Still others are studying environmental factors such as viral infections, metabolic imbalances and exposure to certain chemicals (www.autism-society.org).

Often, family members of persons on the autism spectrum have mild autistic traits. Some of these traits include visual thinking, strong intellectual abilities, shyness, and learning disabilities. Other conditions that are often present in individuals with autism or their families are depression, anxiety, attention deficit disorder, Tourette's syndrome, and alcoholism (Narayan, Moyes, & Wolff, 1990; www.ninds.nih.gov). Common symptoms include sensory sensitivities, hyperactivity and anxiety. Some excellent resources on autism include Tony Attwood's *Asperger's Syndrome: A Guide for Parents and Professionals* (2008), and the web pages for organizations such as the Autism Society of America (www. autism-society.org), the Center for the Study of Autism (www.autism.org), the National Institutes of Health (www.nih.gov), and the Mayo Foundation for Medical Education and Research (www.mayoclinic.com).

Types of Autism

Not all children or adults on the autism spectrum have all of the symptoms discussed here and are not diagnosed with the classical form of autism with speech delay. Those with behavior problems such as social awkwardness who do not have language problems often are diagnosed with autism with no speech delay (level 1). Individuals with this milder type of autism tend to function more comfortably in the community and demonstrate more typical thinking and speech patterns. Yet, both groups have difficulty with flexible problem solving, social interactions, facial recognition, and fine-motor coordination, for example. People on the autism spectrum may act very differently from each other, even if they have the same diagnosis.

The more severe kind of autism presents with more obvious neurological problems, which include auditory processing deficits and the inability to understand speech. Individuals with this kind of autism may not be able to hear complex speech sounds; some cannot follow simple commands. Even though a pure-tone hearing test may yield normal results, the child or adult may not be able to understand speech. Hearing the consonant sounds may be especially difficult. In severe cases, the child may hear only vowels. My speech teacher helped me hear the consonants by stretching them out and enunciating them. She would hold up a cup and say, "ccccupppp." When grownups talked fast, I could not understand them. For a long time, I thought grownups had a special "grownup" language.

A number of individuals with this form of autism also show signs of subtle seizures such as staring or "spacing out." Others experience a mixing of sensory channels. For example, sounds may come through as color or touch as a sound-like sensation (Cesaroni & Garber, 1991). Some individuals simply do not know where their body boundaries are. Many are considered low functioning and have low IQ scores. Some have developmental disabilities and a lower IQ, but others simply have serious sensory processing problems that make communication difficult.

Of course, the less severely affected the person with autism is, the more complex the job he or she can usually hold. For example, I know college professors, business owners and engineers on the autism spectrum who go to work every day and manage themselves quite well. Regardless, the outside world is usually not a welcoming place for those of us with such acute differences from the norm, primarily because our sensory and nervous systems are often pretty raw. Noises too loud and sudden, touch too strong or too soft, smells too intense, tastes too extreme, and visuals too stimulating can send us over the edge—or shut us down into withdrawal.

Yet, we are not all alike, for as mentioned earlier, autism affects people differently. Popular opinion paints those on the autism spectrum as having little emotional contact with the outside world, including not making eye contact, showing affection, smiling or laughing. But this is an overgeneralization and, like most other generalizations, is not entirely factual. It is true that many withdraw, but just like others, they respond to their environment in both positive and negative ways. When we are tired, we might feel disjointed, a bit lost. With enough sleep, you'll find us laughing with coworkers, enjoying a sunny day, or a quiet time with our family.

Major Challenges

The challenges people on the autism spectrum face can include all or some of the following:

- *Problems with social skills and developing friendships.* This occurs for a variety of reasons. Often the person on the spectrum hyper-focuses on favorite subjects, talking non-stop about them and missing social cues from others to stop. Sometimes people on the spectrum tune out others when they find themselves becoming overstimulated or anxious. Individuals may act aloof, keeping themselves apart from others as a way to manage their anxieties. As a result, they can appear unfriendly, sometimes even rude.

- *Difficulty in carrying on conversations.* This challenge is fairly common for people on the spectrum. Because our interests can be obscure, they may not be interesting to others. But often, that doesn't stop us from talking on and on about them.

- *No receptive speech.* The most severely affected individuals cannot speak, even though they may have more normal thinking patterns and emotions. Incoming speech sounds may fade in and out, or they may be a jumble of sound.

- *Obsession with rituals or restricted behavioral patterns.* Sameness is very important to people on the autism spectrum. Wearing the same clothing, traveling the same route to work or school each day, and eating the same foods at each meal are common. They may also practice behaviors such as rocking or hand flapping as a way to stimulate or soothe their nervous systems.

- *Sensory problems.* Difficulties in this area occur because an individual's neurological system is not sending and processing messages in a smooth, even manner. Smells that are too strong or textures that are too rough, for example, can upset the sensory system to the point that an individual becomes irritated and overwhelmed.

- *Fine- and gross-motor difficulties.* These problems are also related to the sensory system, which fails to send the proper messages to the muscular system. As a result, the person may be uncoordinated, drop things, and even fall down easily.

- *Difficulty understanding others' thoughts.* This means it can be difficult for individuals on the spectrum to read social, facial, and other important behavioral cues. The world is a "social" place, and all sorts of problems can occur when you can't tell that people around you are upset with your behavior or uncomfortable about the topic you are discussing with them. I have gotten into a lot of trouble at jobs for bluntly criticizing others' work or showing up in inappropriate clothing for the workplace. It took several concerned mentors to help me figure my way through the fallout from those situations.

- *Tantrums.* Life can be so confusing and upsetting for people on the autism spectrum that they tantrum when they become overwhelmed. As a youngster, I would tantrum when I became frustrated with my inability to communicate verbally with my family. It is a way, although not a very effective one, to let off steam built up from an overload of anxieties and frustrations.

- *Theory of mind.* Often people on the autism spectrum have a difficult time understanding that others may have different ideas on subjects or may disagree with them about a subject. For example, I once wrote a letter to the president of the company at which I was working that essentially said his employees had done a horrible job of installing some equipment. He was furious and horribly embarrassed, of course, which I could not understand at the time. Once again, my mentors stepped in to help me understand the situation—and save my job!

- *Anxiety.* For many of us, anxiety is a major problem, especially when dealing with a new situation. Our nervous systems seem rawer than those of others who are not on the autism spectrum. Sometimes using more than one sensory channel will cause us to shut down. For instance, some may not understand speech if they are focusing on the speaker's facial expression. Others may not notice physical sensations if they are listening to somebody talk at the same time. This overload can lead to anxiety, sometimes even panic attacks.

- *Depression and other emotional problems.* Life can be so difficult and confusing for people with autism spectrum disorders that they end up suffering from depression and other serious emotional problems. Just as these disorders can wreak havoc in nonautistic individuals' lives, they can have a devastating effect on those with ASD. Thankfully, there are now wonderful medications and other treatments that can help alleviate some of the effects of these problems.

In the next chapter we will look at how to manage some of the most salient characteristics of autism spectrum disorders in the workplace to help you secure and maintain a job.

CHAPTER 2

Easing into the Workplace

I n order for many on the autism spectrum to join the workforce, their sensory sensitivities must be "smoothed," communication skills built, and anxiety reduced through treatment and, sometimes, medication. In the following, we will take a closer look at the major sensory issues affecting survival in the world of work and ways to cope.

The Sensory System

The sensory system helps the body maintain equilibrium in a very complex world. It brings vital information from the outside world into our inside world. In a typical working nervous system, information flows smoothly through the nervous system into the brain, which acts as a traffic cop of sorts. That is, the brain tells the appropriate body part to move, stop doing what it is doing, slow down, and so on.

A person with ASD has trouble processing information from the outside world because sensory problems literally make it difficult to understand what is being seen, heard, and touched. It's as if there is no volume control in the incoming sensory stimuli. Sounds that would not bother neurotypical persons can make you feel as if you were inside the speakers at a booming rock concert. Sounds such as those coming from a smoke alarm hurt like a dentist drill hitting a nerve.

That is, in most individuals with autism spectrum disorders the sensory system does not work in an organized fashion. Instead, sensory messages may course through the nervous system, bombarding the brain with an overload of information, or too little information, which can be just as bad. It's as if there are detours everywhere, sending the nerve signals off on tangents, down dead ends and through unmarked roads. The result can be a lot of anxiety, confusion and subsequently upset or irritable behaviors for both children and adults with autism. Upset behavior for adults translates into irritability, withdrawal, anxiety, confusion, and even anger.

A simple way to determine if a child or adult has severe sensory problems is to watch his/her reaction at a busy supermarket. If every trip results in a screaming tantrum, it is safe to conclude that sensory overload is the cause. Sensory problems on the autism spectrum are very variable from person to person. Some have mild problems; for others, they are severe. In some individuals, the problems are mainly auditory and, in others, mainly visual. Nonverbal persons may experience severe sensory scrambling in both the visual and auditory systems. They may "hear" something, but perceive the communication visually, or they may be "seeing" something and experience it auditorily. Their problems are in the brain; the eyes and ears are usually normal.

Although all human beings suffer from the above symptoms at times, people on the autism spectrum generally suffer from them more often and intensely. Luckily, there are ways to manage so they occur less frequently—and rarely at work. After a general overview, we will examine the following sensory sensitivities: auditory, visual, tactile, and smell.

Sensory Problems on the Job

Individuals with severe sensory problems often have difficulty with the work environment. A talented computer programmer I know quit his job because he could not stand the noise in the office. Making the workplace tolerable for individuals with severe sensory oversensitivity usually requires some simple modifications in the environment along with the person with autism spectrum disorders trying to reduce his or her sensitivities. Success is more likely if both of these approaches are used.

Let me use myself as an example. Loud high-pitched noises can startle me and make me lose my train of thought. I teach on the college level, but I could never teach a class of very young children because their high-pitched voices and quick movements would make me crazy. My fine-motor skills aren't too bad, but I know others on the spectrum who can barely write, and, for sure, should never be near a hammer and nails. If I'm in a crowd where everyone is talking at once, I won't be able to hear the person with whom I am conversing—or the rest of the people, for that matter. If their voices are of different pitches, I'll tune everyone out even faster.

Smells don't bother me too much, but they are a problem for many on the spectrum. Can you imagine being sensitive to smell and having to sit next to a woman wearing strong perfume at a meeting? You wouldn't hear or see any of the meeting because all you could think of was escaping the smell. Then, once you did, you would feel so sick you couldn't concentrate for the rest of the day.

For reasons like these, it is easy to see how the average American workplace could cause sensory overload for some of us on the autism spectrum—unless we go to work prepared to modulate our senses, and, of course, our reactions to stress. See Table 2.1 for some ways to manage these sensitivities.

Table 2.1:
Sensory Sensitivities and How to Manage Them

Sensory Sensitivity	Problem	Solution
Auditory Sensitivity	Difficulty modulating sounds	• Wear earplugs • Listen to music through headphones • Turn down telephone ringer volume • Have "white noise" such as a fan's whirring, indoor fountain or environmental music in background • Record offending sound and gradually get used to it through exposure • Sometimes a noisy tool or device can be better tolerated if the autistic person turns it on and off many times.
	Difficulty understanding spoken messages and other sounds	• Write down oral messages as you hear them • Rely on written communications • Chew gum to help auditory focus
Visual Sensitivity	Fluorescent or LED lighting's buzzing and flickering is irritating, distracting	• Wear a hat with a brim • Put desk near window for better natural lighting • Find an LED light that does not flicker and put it on your desk • Wear tinted glasses • Use laptop computer (less flickering on screen) or flat-screen desktop computer (also less flickering)

Table 2.1 *continued*

Sensory Sensitivity	Problem	Solution
Visual Sensitivity *(continued)*	Can't find papers, objects (not processing visual information fast enough)	• Provide visual structure through color coding of files • Keep the files of current projects on or near your desk for easy reach. Keep old files in a file cabinet away from the desk so they don't clutter the area
	Harsh contrast between light is distracting	• Copy reading materials on tan, light gray, light blue or green paper to reduce contrast. Use colored overlays over reading material or tinted glasses
	Seeing people walk by is distracting	• Move work area out of heavily trafficked areas • Have desk face wall instead of hallway
Tactile Sensitivity	Light touch is irritating and distracting	• Wear soft clothing without tags • Buy clothes from thrift store because they are usually softer than new ones
Smell Sensitivity	Smells nauseate or make dizzy	• Chew peppermint or cinnamon gum to cover up smell or have scent diffuser with green apple scent for focus, vanilla or lavender for calming, and peppermint for energizing nervous system • Ask nearby workmates not to wear strong perfume

Table 2.1 *continued*

Sensory Sensitivity	Problem	Solution
Anger or Anxiety at Work	Lose temper easily	• Practice de-stressing techniques (for example, deep breathing, calming ritual after work) • Eat crunchy or chewy foods to calm the nervous system and sour or strong foods such as lemon drops or peppermint to energize nervous system • Get aerobic exercise • Leave confrontations before they escalate • Problem solve with supervisor/ colleagues • Use diplomacy • Pay attention to others' body language • Practice relaxation techniques such as deep breathing, visualization • Cultivate allies at work • Use medication, if appropriate • Avoid discussing controversial subjects • Switch from anger to crying

From S. Banker. (2003). Personal interview. Children's Therapy Group, Overland Park, Kansas.

Sound Sensitivity

For many on the spectrum, sound sensitivity is a huge issue. It certainly is for me. When I was a child, my hearing was so sensitive that it was as though my ears were a microphone amplifying the sounds around me. My hearing tests as normal, but I can't modulate incoming sounds. So I have two choices: (a) turn on my hearing and be deluged with sound or (b) shut off my hearing. Needless to say, neither of these options works in all situations, especially in the workplace. My sound sensitivity problems have become less severe in adulthood, but many individuals have severe sound sensitivity problems for their whole life.

The typical workplace is full of different kinds of sounds and pitches that can be distracting and uncomfortable, sometimes downright painful: fire alarms, squealing microphone feedback, chairs scraping the floor, along with all the coworkers' and others' voices. For example, I can't hear on the phone in a busy airport or a noisy office due to the distractions, and continuous sounds.

Before they even hear the dreaded sound, many children on the autism spectrum misbehave if they fear a noise is going to occur; adults, on the other hand, may become withdrawn or irritable when they are apprehensive about noises (Williams et al., 2021). They appear to go into the "fright, fight, or flight" mode.

What to Do

Wearing earplugs can help mute the distracting and loud noises at work, but they should never be worn all day to prevent the sensory system from "over-accommodating" for the diluted sounds. That is, wearing earplugs all the time may make sound sensitivity worse. Listening to music through headphones can block out unwanted sounds and help maintain a relaxed attitude. Occupational therapist Sarah Banker, OTR/L, (2003) suggests covering up irritating sounds with a relaxing sound such as "white noise" or water from a small indoor fountain. For some, a fan's whirring is calming, a kind of white noise itself. Another solution would be to play environmental music at work, if permitted and appropriate. Some mobile phones have ringers that are difficult to tolerate. Changing the ring on the phones in the vicinity may help.

Persons with auditory-processing problems, that is, an inability to properly understand, comprehend and process information that is heard, usually have difficulty understanding spoken messages as well as responding to other sounds at the same time. Banker (2003) suggests they rely on written messages for most of their communication but also write down oral messages as they listen to them. In addition, she says, chewing gum may also help concentration and makes remembering messages easier.

Autistic people can often learn to tolerate a loud sound better if they control it. For example, to tolerate machinery noises, they should find a time to turn the noisy tool on and off many times. Another method that may help reduce sound sensitivity is making a recording of the offending sound. The person plays the recording back at a very low volume and gradually increases it. The person must control both the volume and the length of time the sound is played.

Visual Sensitivity

Probably the biggest visual problem in the workplace is fluorescent lighting. Not only does the buzzing sound bother many on the autism spectrum, so does the light's constant flickering, which otherwise goes unnoticed by most. Researchers have reported that fluorescent lighting can increase the repetitive behavior of some children on the autism spectrum (Coleman, Frankel, Ritvo, & Freeman, 1976).

What to Do

LED lights that flicker can be really distressing to some individuals on the autism spectrum. Some LEDs flicker and others do not. To find the bad flickering LEDs, video the room in slow motion. To a person who is sensitive to the flicker, it makes the room look like a disco with strobe lights. If fixing the lights is not possible, try the following:

- Wear a hat
- Move the person's workstation near a window
- If the workplace has no windows, place a strong LED light that does not flicker on the person's desk

The use of either a laptop or a tablet will solve the problem with flickering computer monitors. Some flat screens flicker and others do not. Try increasing the screen refresh rate if a large flat screen monitor flickers.

Irlen-tinted lenses have helped some people with visual sensitivity. Developed by Helen Irlen, these lenses have especially helped people with problems perceiving their surroundings and difficulty reading (Irlen, 1991). These glasses help their wearers feel more relaxed, be less bothered by bright lighting, and be less distracted by perceptual distortions that can throw off their motor coordination. A person must choose the color lens that works best for him or her. Another option is to choose from the different tinted glasses in pale colors available at local sunglass stores. I find the pale pinks, purples, and browns are helpful. Even though many claim that colored lenses help them, Irlen lenses are generally considered a controversial therapy as their effectiveness has not been empirically validated.

Occupational therapist Banker (2003) suggests people wear dark-tinted glasses, adjust the brightness of their computer screens or, better yet, replace TV-type monitors with flat-screen monitors, which do not flicker as much. The best screens are either laptops or tablets. The screen on these devices never flicker.

Smell Sensitivities

Smells can be quite distracting to people on the autism spectrum and, although this sensitivity is not as common as some of the others discussed here, it can still make life difficult. Imagine becoming nauseated or dizzy every time the person in the next workstation used hand lotion, ate a garlicky dish for lunch, or simply had a case of bad breath. The smell of perfume is obnoxious for some; others may not be bothered by it at all.

What to Do

One easy way to reduce the discomforts of smell is to chew gum, for the mint or cinnamon smell of the gum will float around the nose level covering up other unpleasant smells, Banker (2003) says. Another approach is to use some of the many products on the market specifically designed to cover up odors. For example, Banker points out that green apple scent is good for focus, vanilla and lavender are calming, and peppermint is energizing. Candles also work well to diffuse troubling smells but since they are forbidden in most workplaces for safety reasons, using a scent diffuser is best. In some cases, it may be possible to ask a coworker to not wear the offending perfume at work.

Other Tools

Listening Therapies

One treatment for helping some people with sensory problems is "listening therapy," which relies on specially modulated music to desensitize the sensory system. However, it does not work for everyone. This is one of the challenges when dealing with autism—a treatment that works for one does not necessarily work for another.

Benefits of listening programs (auditory training) for some individuals include:

- Reducing sound sensitivity
- Improving receptive and expressive language
- Reducing stress from sensory overload

The Alert Program

The Alert Program teaches people of all ages how to regulate their sensory systems using techniques developed over the years by occupational therapists. The Alert Program was created by occupational therapists Mary Sue Williams and Sherry Shellenberger, whose 1996 book, *How Does Your Engine Run? A Leader's Guide to the Alert Program for Self-Regulation*, describes in detail the strategies for changing or maintaining states of alertness as well as the underlying theory of sensory integration (www. alertprogram.com). The program teaches participants first how to track their energy level and then how to slow themselves down or speed themselves up, depending on the situation. For example, if you need to calm down and focus your thoughts, you could stretch your arms against a wall and do a few quick arm push-ups. Right before you take a test, reach out with your arms across your body to energize both sides of the brain.

Controlling Anger

A major problem for many people on the spectrum is modulating emotions. Because of their sensory processing problems, they often feel frustrated and angry. With so much stimulation coming at them, they may feel as if their environment is out of their control. Some lose their cool and lash out, whereas others become anxious and shut down. Either way, the emotional ups and downs can be a major problem for the individual with ASD as well as for those around.

Losing your temper at work is threatening and frightening to your colleagues. Shutting down and not communicating is also a problem when you are in the workplace. Neither one will be tolerated for long, especially in these tense and violence-wary times. One of the major reasons people get fired from a job is their failure to get along with others. So knowing what to do when you are finding yourself losing control is a major part of your life education.

Anger outbursts won't be tolerated, either in school or the workplace. In short, if you hit somebody or throw a computer, you are fired. After getting in several fistfights in high school when other students teased me, I learned to control my anger by switching my emotion from anger to crying. I had to learn to control my temper because I had been kicked out of a large high school for throwing a book at a girl who teased me. Similarly, at the boarding school I attended, horseback riding was taken away after I got into a fistfight.

After that I switched my emotion from anger to crying. As a result, when I had a problem with a coworker, I hid in the cattle corral and cried. Crying is tolerated at work— intense anger is not. I learned that anger for me was like a snarling lion in a cage. It is too dangerous to open the cage door even one inch because if the lion shoves the door open, I cannot control him.

I have worked at many meat plants on new equipment installation. It is normal during installations of equipment for things to go wrong and to lose production time. Plant managers who have never experienced a major equipment installation often think the new equipment will work perfectly in the first five minutes. On several projects, when things went wrong, the plant manager screamed at me. To prevent losing my temper, I looked at him as if he were a two-year-old having a tantrum because he thinks I broke his toy. I used to call this the tantrum phrase of new equipment startups. In these instances, I calmly took the manager by the hand and led him back to the conference room and explained to him that his plant was not broken and that some loss of production was normal.

I then told him about other equipment startups that went really badly and reassured him that the startup in his plant was going well compared to other plants. There were other times I was yelled at while operating a new piece of equipment and just kept operating the equipment without responding. After the manager left, I went out into the cattle corrals and cried.

Throughout my career, I have never had an anger incident that would have jeopardized my job as I deliberately developed a way to deal with difficult situations that I knew would upset me.

What to Do
You must develop strategies for controlling anger if you want to keep your job. It is easier for a girl to switch to crying than for a guy, but crying is still preferable to getting fired, no matter who you are. There may be coworkers who deliberately try to provoke you. If that happens, this may be a good time to talk to your boss and possibly switch your workstation or transfer to another department or area. Another tactic is to cultivate powerful allies who can help you deal with a mean coworker.

As a general rule, avoid discussing controversial religious, political or sexual topics at work. Opinionated views on these subjects can make coworkers dislike you. There are times when you have to politely say that you are feeling stressed and have to go outside to calm down. Always leave the confrontation before it escalates. Also, you may have an easier time controlling anger if you get plenty of aerobic exercise. Vigorous exercise calms down the nervous system and helps you focus.

In addition to medication, as discussed below, meditation and relaxation exercises can help control anger and other strong emotions. Both meditation and relaxation exercises can be done at work. Find an empty room or a bench outside where you can go when you feel you are going to lose your temper. If you do blow up, you must go outside and get away from your coworkers immediately before you end up doing something violent or saying something you will regret later. In today's world, there is zero tolerance for violent behavior.

Medication

Medication is one of the tools used increasingly to modulate sensory system problems and control depression and anxiety. In recent years we have learned much about the brain and a host of medications have been developed that can help people on the autism spectrum to lead more typical and productive lives. Managing one's challenges through medication is a decision that needs to be taken very seriously. When considering this option, start out by finding a competent doctor. Ask for recommendations from people you know in support groups, for example.

Medication has worked well for me for many years. As I wrote in Thinking in Pictures (2006), I became very anxious when I entered puberty, and those anxieties intensified as I grew older. Others may have a few problems at puberty and then calm down and never need medication to deal with their problems. My anxiety made me feel as if

I were in a constant state of "stage fright." I lived with this anxiety disorder until I turned 34 and went through eye surgery, which intensified my anxieties even more. I read as much as I could about possible biochemical answers to my problem before asking my doctor to prescribe an antidepressant that researchers had discovered decreased anxieties.

Within two days, I could feel a difference. I have come to realize that without the antidepressant, my body is in a constant state of physiological vigilance, ready to flee nonexistent predators. That is common for many on the autism spectrum, due to our sensitive nervous systems. But it is also true for many nonautistic individuals who suffer from depression and anxiety, and whose nervous systems are biologically prepared for flight.

After three years I switched to another antidepressant, which was in the same family of medications but has had fewer side effects for me. Today there are even more choices of medications for people on the autism spectrum with generally even fewer side effects such as dry mouth and constipation. The newest SSRIs (Selective Serotonin Reuptake Inhibitors) are preferred.

Although medication can be a lifesaver for many on the autism spectrum, the wrong dose—or the wrong medication—can wreak havoc. I have heard many horror stories of how giving the wrong drug to someone on the autism spectrum with epilepsy can cause grand mal seizures, or how too high a dose of antidepressant sent the person into a rage.

What to Do

The general rule for medications for those on the spectrum is to start off low and stay low. According to Dr. Paul Hardy, an autism specialist in Boston, and Dr. John Ratey, a psychiatrist with the Harvard Medical School, people with autism often require lower doses of antidepressants than nonautistic people due to abnormal development of serotonin systems in the brain (Hardy, 1989; Ratey et al., 1987). Some only need one fourth to one third of the normal dose. Too high of a dose causes agitation, aggression, excitability, with insomnia being the first symptom if the dose is not correct. When these symptoms occur, the antidepressant must either be stopped or the dose must be reduced (Hardy, 1989; Ratey et al., 1987). Such decisions should always be made in consultation with one's physician.

People on the autism spectrum sometimes use Risperdal to control rage and aggression. Again, Dr. Joe Huggins, an autism specialist in Canada, found that the dose must be kept very low for people on the spectrum (Huggins, 1995). Sometimes a combination of medication, diet, and a sensory treatment is more effective than any one treatment alone.

Donna Williams, the author of *Nobody Nowhere and Somebody Somewhere* (1992), described very severe visual problems. In addition, her sound sensitivity problems were so severe that she could not even tolerate clapping at a conference. Today a combination of a casein- and gluten-free diet, Irlen lenses and a tiny dose of Risperdal makes it possible for her to tolerate being in a large convention hall. When I saw her at a convention recently, she was the new Donna. The combination of conventional medicines and alternative treatments was very successful. For Donna, Risperdal helped reduce her sensory problems, but it was also essential for her to continue her special diet.

Be open-minded and try different things. Some are helped by vitamin supplements such as B6 and magnesium dimethylglycine (DMG), or Omega 3 supplements. Information on the DAN (Defeat Autism Now) protocol can be obtained from Dr. Bernard Rimland's Autism Research Institute in San Diego (www.autism. com). It contains information on diets and supplements that may be helpful.

Medication should never be considered the only tool for helping a person on the autism spectrum lead a fruitful life. Teaching and coaching life skills is a critical part of the treatment. Exercise, too, is extremely helpful in calming a person down. For me, exercise has helped reduce my anxiety and improve my sleep. Not only does it tone the body, it also produces endorphins—brain chemicals that help you feel good and stay focused.

Whatever you decide about medication, make sure you read about the different types and work with an experienced doctor to determine which type would be best for you. Sometimes you will have to try several to find the one that works the best. Don't be put off by that, for that is part of making a good decision about your life. (The expanded edition of *Thinking in Pictures* contains an extensive update on medications; Grandin, 2006). The information in this book is still accurate. During the last 15 years, there have been few changes in the medication.

Social Skills for the Workplace

Employers will tell you that one of the major reasons people don't do well in the workplace is that they can't get along with their colleagues. This is a big problem for everybody but can be devastating for those of us with autism spectrum disorders. To keep the workplace running smoothly, people have to get along. There's no way around it, so figuring out how to do so is an important part of your education. Oddly enough, work-related social problems are often less severe for people on the spectrum who have more obvious disabilities, such as no speech. Once other employees understand autism, they are often very helpful. It is the people who are closer to being typical who have the worst problems with office politics and jealousy.

Getting in trouble socially is a big problem for individuals on the autism spectrum. Many people with autism are socially naïve, expecting everybody to be honest and kind. It can be a rude awakening to discover there are some people in the world who might exploit us. Ideally, your employer should let your fellow employees know about your autism, so they can be more understanding and forgiving of some of our more eccentric traits—our fixation on certain subjects and sometimes odd dress. Of course, that assumes you have disclosed your disability.

That brings up a whole other issue: whether or not to self-disclose. In many technical fields, people with autism or autistic-like behaviors are very common, and it may be better to avoid disclosure. In fields that require more social skills, disclosure may be advisable (see the Appendix for more information).

Some autistic strengths can be a problem on the job. For example, our ability to focus intently can mean it's difficult for us to make transitions. That kind of focus can also make it difficult to supervise others, especially if there is a lot of customer and colleague contact. I know one fellow who had worked successfully for a number of years at an architectural firm only to lose his job after he was promoted to a position that required a great deal of customer contact. Also, during conferences I have talked to highly skilled people on the autism spectrum who lost good jobs when they were promoted into management.

In response to this problem, some engineering firms are changing their policies to allow their good "techies" to advance along a "techie" track and not ruin them by making them managers. Related to the same issue, Massachusetts Institute for Technology (MIT), the famous engineering university, now offers social skills classes. Many engineers have autistic traits. A study by Simon Baron-Cohen (2000) in England indicated that there were twice as many engineers in the family histories of people on the autism spectrum. That is certainly true for me. My grandfather was an MIT-trained engineer who was a co-inventor of the automatic pilot for airplanes.

Getting Along with Others

Probably the most important social skill to learn is knowing how to read coworkers' emotions and social cues. I have heard a number of stories of people on the autism spectrum losing their jobs because they did not recognize that their coworkers either did not like them or were jealous of their talents.

One person was fired because his employer discovered pornography on his computer. The guy was innocent; presumably, a jealous or angry coworker planted the offensive materials. In other cases, I have had unhappy employees break equipment I had just installed in my clients' livestock facilities. In less extreme situations, you simply have to learn to deal with the ups and downs of your coworkers' lives, some of whom would like to spend way too much time describing their personal problems. You need to share some of those life experiences with each other, but too much of it makes the workplace become a tense, unhappy place.

What to Do

When I begin work with a new client, I pay attention to the body language of the employees on whose "turf" I'll be treading. Look for the people at meetings who sit with their arms crossed, are particularly silent, or act unfriendly toward you. In my line of work, it's usually not the plant manager or superintendent or hourly worker who are jealous; it's more often the head maintenance person or engineer, who does a job similar to mine who acts in a passive-aggressive manner. You might find this person moving very slowly while working on your project with you, or perhaps she simply refuses to show up to help at a crucial time in the installation. Whatever the situation, there are always a million ways to mess up the job.

What can you do about this? Make a point of getting to know those people in order to defuse their anger or concern about their job. Ask for their opinion and bring them into the work you are doing as much as possible. Talk with them about their family, get to know their life and share your own experiences with them. They may feel threatened because an outsider has been hired to do what they may consider "their job." If that does not help, talk with your supervisor about the problem. Knowing how to "talk" with coworkers, clients and customers is also key to staying on the job. Tom McKean, author of *Soon Will Come the Light* (1994), told about an experience he had with a computer programming professor who flunked him for finding a better way of writing a program. Tom would walk up to the board and erase and correct his professor's example. I'm sure Tom's direct manner and speech are what caused the problem. I'm just as sure, however, that a more creative professor could have found a way to incorporate Tom's criticisms into the class discussion. Knowing how to disagree with those in command is an important lesson to be learned.

Early in my career, when I was working with a large feedlot construction company, I sold a contract to a meat-packing plant to design and build a new cattle ramp. During construction, I tactlessly criticized some workmen's sloppy welding. The plant engineer pulled me aside and advised me to apologize before a small problem turned into a major one. I went to the cafeteria and apologized to the staff and in the process learned a great lesson about how to talk about problems with others.

If you see a problem occurring on the job, don't attack the person or his work. Instead, engage the employee in a conversation about the job. If you can get him talking about what he is doing, he might notice the mistakes he is making and rectify them.

But I didn't entirely learn the lesson, for a year later I got into a tussle with the president of the company, to whom I had written a letter criticizing the sloppy installation of some equipment at another plant. The letter embarrassed the company president because it made him look as if he ran a sloppy organization. This time it was the plant manager who bailed me out. He turned out to be one of my most important workplace mentors.

One of the greatest lessons I learned from this manager was that talent earns respect. When I first arrived at the plant, I was literally a pain. I talked way too much, probably drove him crazy, but he tolerated me because I was able to come up with some pretty clever ways to solve problems, such as using plastic milk hoses to pad gate edges and prevent the livestock from bruising.

If you are talented, you can often get away with being eccentric at work, but you usually can't get away with poor grooming—a very important part of social skills. To be out among others, you have to fit in as much as possible, and that includes the way you groom yourself. You don't have to look like everyone else, but you must not be a slob. At one of my first jobs, the construction manager, another one of my mentors, got his department secretaries to take me shopping for clothes. He was very blunt about what I had to do socially to be successful at the company, including wearing deodorant. I did not like him talking to me like that at the time, but later I realized that he had done me a huge favor.

Having mentors is an excellent way to learn the social rules of the workplace. Thanks to them and just plain experience, I have grown more tactful and diplomatic over the years. I have learned to never go over the head of the person who hired me unless I have his or her permission. The first lesson I had to learn was that I could not tell other people that they were stupid. I know several people on the autism spectrum who were fired because they told their boss that he was stupid.

Talent Earns Respect

It is our tendency to pinpoint the negative, to find the faults because they upset our sense of order. In general, look for the good things your colleagues and boss are doing on the job. That way when there are problems, you can balance them out with the positive. On one job, the plant engineer had installed the hydraulics wrong, and, as a result, we had to tear it out and rebuild it. I helped smooth his rumpled feathers by complimenting him on his beautiful electric panels. His electrical work deserved a compliment.

Learn as much diplomacy as you can before you enter the work world. Observe others, how they get along with each other. Read about talented people to find out how they got along in the world. For myself, I learned about diplomacy by reading about international negotiations and using them as models. In many situations, I just avoid the people who would cause trouble. I can usually tell who they are by their body language and facial expressions. They sit stiffly, with their arms folded and do not change their facial expressions.

Recently, a woman with autism made the following reply to my advice: "Honesty is the best way." I told her that you can still be honest without giving your opinion about everything. I told her that you were hired to do a job, not criticize the boss or your coworkers. If you have to correct somebody's mistake, say something like, "If you do it this way, it will work better."

Other advice includes refraining from gossiping and never writing e-mail containing personal information that is critical of coworkers or your boss. Never write nasty emails about the boss or coworkers you do not like. Many people have been fired due to inappropriate things they write in e-mail. If you want to have a private discussion with one of your coworkers about a problem in the office, do not use email. Go out for lunch or sit in a park. When you delete email, it doesn't go away. The boss can retrieve it off the server. At one company an employee was fired because he wrote an email that said that when his boss got mad, his face looked like a "putrid, quivering pumpkin."

Another thing that can get you into trouble is gossiping about other employees. Don't do it. I talked to one lady who was a good employee but got into trouble by talking about sensitive subjects at work. Unless a person is a very close friend, it is best to avoid topics such as sex, religion and politics. Much safer subjects are sports, movies, hobbies, work-related conversation, the weather and what you did on the weekend. Extreme views on religion or politics can really turn off coworkers.

Problems with the Boss

A change of boss can cause problems for anybody—with or without autism spectrum disorders. I have met several people on the autism spectrum who had stable employment until a boss who appreciated their talents left the company. When they got a new boss, their lives became miserable, and some even lost their jobs. Tyrants who get into power make life miserable for everybody. During a 50-year consulting career, I have worked on long complex projects with about 100 companies. I have seen some very good bosses but also some bad bosses who not only made their employees' lives miserable but also did great damage to their companies.

There are two types of bad bosses. The first type is terrible for everybody. The second type may get along with the "neurotypical" people but does not like the "weird" autistic person. I had a problem with the second type when the magazine I worked for got a new manager. Jim, the new manager, thought I was weird and wanted to get rid of me.

I was too socially inept to know what was going on, but my friend Sue in the graphics department cautioned me and subsequently helped me assemble a portfolio of articles I had written. When Jim saw the portfolio, he recognized the value of my work and, instead of firing me, he gave me a raise.

Other situations do not work out as well. There are some people who will never get along. If you work for a large corporation or a government agency, you may be able to get transferred if you are in a situation where you do not get along with somebody, but if you work for a small company you are in trouble unless you become friendly with your colleagues and gain their support.

In some situations employees on and off the autism spectrum have no choice but to learn to work with a difficult boss. This does not lead to productive employees, but people tolerate it when jobs are scarce and they need a paycheck. The workplace is just like any other organization in your life: There is good and there is bad, and you just have to take both.

Organizational Skills at Work

Being organized at work is difficult for most people. We don't do a good job of teaching our children these very important skills. For someone on the autism spectrum, having strong organizational skills is an absolute must. They make work better, smoother, and more fulfilling. In some cases, they can mean the difference between keeping a job and losing it.

The Big Picture

To be successful on the job, everyone, autistic and non-autistic alike, needs a plan and a daily structure. There are lots of books written about this subject, so this discussion will be short.

To start off, people need to keep in mind what's important to them in life. That sounds like a huge process, but it doesn't have to be. In his book *Seven Habits of Highly Effective People* (1990), Stephen Covey advises people to write a personal mission statement that will govern how they make choices. People start this process, Covey writes, by asking what they want the different people in their lives—family, friends, neighbors, clients and colleagues—to say about them at their funerals. That is, what they want to be remembered for. For most of us, it's something nice: How kind we are to others, how great we are at certain tasks, and so on.

For example, perhaps it's important for you to become an excellent photographer, to learn as much as you can about taking memorable pictures and having them exhibited in art galleries in your hometown. This goal would then become an overriding focus in your life, one you would support daily by selecting goals that would help you achieve that purpose. In other words, every step you take, every choice you make, must support that goal in your life.

Role	Goal
Photographer	1. Enroll in university class 2. Practice 3. Enter local photography contest 4. Read photography trade journal 5. Attend local photographers' meeting and make 3 new contacts

Let that be the starting point, Covey writes, for how you decide what roles are important in life. Once the roles are decided, you select the goals for each role and plug them into a weekly calendar. It's important, Covey suggests, to plan a week at a time in order to see life's big picture. However, depending on the job, you might plan even further out or less.

Day to Day

Thom Hartman, a psychologist who writes about attention deficit disorder, also suggests people write down their goals and create timelines and other plans for how to reach those goals. In his book, *Focus Your Energy: Hunting for Success in Business with Attention Deficit Disorder* (1994), Hartman suggests that people surround themselves with written reminders of their goals so they can visualize them and make them more concrete. Hartman also recommends the following organizational strategy for prioritizing work commitments.

To keep track of schedules, you need a big calendar on which to write project dates and appointments. I cannot use any of the new fancy electronic calendars because I have to write the information out in order to remember it. Something concrete and visual works best for most of us on the spectrum. I need a calendar where I can see the entire month. This prevents me from mixing up my schedule. It also makes it easier to look at work that will occur several days or weeks ahead.

Since sequencing is one part of organization that is especially difficult for me as a visual thinker, I have to write everything down to keep track of what I am doing. Even today I have problems remembering a sequence to operate a new piece of equipment such as a copy machine. So I have to write down all the steps in the right order.

I had trouble operating the fax machine when the written directions were removed from the machine. All I need is a list of the sequence. In the same way, all the features in mobile phones baffle me. I cannot remember which buttons to push because they are not labeled. I still prefer to use an answering service where an operator reads my messages to me and I have time to write them down. I like the phone system in hotels because getting messages is simple. I just press a button labeled "message." I still have problems getting messages off my mobile phone, so I just rely on the answering service.

To be successful on the job, everyone, autistic and non-autistic alike, needs a plan and a daily structure.

Table 2.2: Prioritizing Work Commitments

1. Make a daily "to-do list" on a legal pad and have two boxes on the desk or work area marked "A" and "B." Label an empty desk drawer "C."

2. Mark everything on the list and every piece of work paper with either "A, B, or C." Do this daily.

3. "A's" are the things that must be done immediately. After defining them, decide the order in which you'll do them. If they are big projects, break them into one- or two-hour blocks of time, which also get marked as "A's." Any papers for "A" projects go into the "A" box.

4. "B's" are next to be done after the "A's" are all finished. Put any "B" papers into the "B" box.

5. Finally, "C's" are least important and therefore get done last. Drop any "C" papers into the "C" drawer.

6. Check your list daily and move up "B's" into "A" slots once those most important projects are completed.

Source: T. Hartman (1994). Focus Your Energy: Hunting for Success in Business with Attention Deficit Disorder. *New York: Pocket Books.*

Being Successful at Work

It takes a lot of interventions for someone on the autism spectrum to be able to be successful at work. Parents must start teaching their children at a young age to be responsible for their belongings and carrying out tasks. As the children grow into adulthood, these lessons will stay with them and help them be more successful—and, I believe, fulfilled in their lives.

In general, a person on the autism spectrum can make a successful transition into work by following these suggestions.

1. *Make gradual transitions*—Start working for short periods while still in high school. The time spent working should gradually be lengthened. I know one mother whose 12-year-old son wants to be a veterinarian, so she takes him to their neighborhood pet store on Saturdays to volunteer for a couple of hours. She stays with him and makes sure that he interacts with customers while he learns how to care for different kinds of animals.

2. *Seek out supportive employers*—Parents and educators should help find employers who are willing to work with people on the autism spectrum. Find employers who appreciate special talents and skills, who need those talents to keep their businesses running. This requires a lot of leg work on parents' part, but the payoff is big. Often community colleges have employment centers for their students and

help build relationships with area employers. Those would be good ones to contact.

3. *Find mentors*—Mentors can help you learn important social and job skills. Mentors also can motivate students to study and introduce them to an interesting job. Mentors can sometimes be found where you least expect it. A good mentor might be the next-door neighbor who works for the power company. This person could get a young person on the spectrum motivated by taking him on a tour of an electric power plant and teaching him how a power plant works, for example. One mother I know called up the local university and paid a biology graduate student to take her son out each weekend. The son and the mentor continued that relationship long after they were both grown and on their own. Schools, churches, and neighborhoods can be good sources for mentors, so can your family. Find a willing uncle or aunt, teacher or neighbor or fellow church member.

Find employers who appreciate special talents and skills, who need those talents to keep their businesses running. People on the autism spectrum have to sell their skills, not themselves, which is the opposite of the way most businesses operate.

4. *Educate employers and employees*—Both employers and coworkers need to be educated about autism spectrum disorders so they can help support the individual. They also need to understand the

person's limitations in terms of social interactions, so as not to push him into situations that could lose him his job.

5. *Consider freelance work*—This is a very good career option for fully verbal individuals with special talents. By working freelance, you can organize your own structure and environment the way it best suits you so as to be more successful. Freelance work also makes it easier to avoid office politics. As a private consultant, I go in and do the job, and then leave. Nevertheless, self-employment can be stressful if it is not handled correctly. There are records to keep, marketing to be done, and clients to keep happy. Make sure you are up for those tasks before deciding to go this route.

6. *Create a portfolio*—People on the autism spectrum have to sell their skills, not themselves, which is the opposite of the way most businesses operate. Because we are not the most social beings, we have to rely heavily on our talents to get work. A portfolio of work allows potential employers or clients to see first-hand the kind of work you do and base their judgment on that and not your personality, which they may find eccentric. It may also allow you to get into the job through the back door, which is how I got all my jobs. If possible, avoid the human resources department and find someone directly in the department where you want to work.

The portfolio can also help a person keep a job. For example, if a new boss finds your social behavior "strange," her opinion may change after viewing a portfolio of your work. Portfolios will not work for every job, however. In those instances, treat your resume or job application as a portfolio and describe in concrete detail the projects, duties and successes you have had on the job. Tell how your talents helped to get a client's project designed and published in less time than the client asked for. Or perhaps you were able to program a new software system that increased your client's business by 25 percent. Be specific and detailed.

7. *Make your own web page to showcase your work*—Web pages are a great way to communicate with potential employers or clients, both of whom need to see proof of your capabilities. In some cases, this works instead of, or in addition to, a portfolio.

8. *Develop skills that other people will value and need*— People thought I was weird, but ranchers need cattle handling facilities and I made myself the very best in designing them. Today there is a huge need for translators of Middle Eastern languages, for example. So if you are good at this skill, you will be hired. I have met several people on the spectrum who became experts in highly specialized fields such as making patterns for leather coats or lighting design for theater. To make up for being considered "strange," you have to make yourself better than others in a

specialized skill that other people need. By the way, no matter how much you like playing video games, video game playing is a skill few employers want!

9. *Keep your career in your talent area*—The minds of people on the spectrum are specialized. You will be good at one thing and not as good at something else. For example, I am good at visual tasks and terrible at foreign languages. Therefore, for me, switching to a translation job would not be wise. A person who is an expert with numbers may be poor at graphic design. I heard a sad story of a successful budget analyst who made a disastrous switch to web page design. He had no design talent.

10. *Get help with financial records and other official record keeping*—Designing complex equipment is easy for me because I can visualize it, but keeping all the paperwork straight on the business end of my free-lance business is a challenge for a visual thinker. As a result, I had to have other people help me set up my corporation and show me how to separate my income from expenses for doing taxes, for example. Many visual thinkers on the spectrum need a reliable person to continuously help them with paperwork and record keeping. Some of the nonvisual thinkers who are trained in accounting may find that keeping records is easy.

Both employers and coworkers need to be educated about autism spectrum disorders so they can help support the individual. Remember to always focus on your talents because they are what will keep you employed.

11. *Manage your temper, anxieties and social skills*—This point may be last on the list, but it is critical to success in the workplace. Nothing will ruin a job faster than somebody losing their cool and blasting their colleagues. If you are going to be out in the world, take care that you do all that you can to be successful in this realm, for it is a difficult area for most of us.

Finally, remember to always focus on your talents because they are what will keep you employed. You will have to prove to people you can do the job asked of you, but with some guidance from family and colleagues, your transition into the workplace will go more smoothly.

Conclusion

To ease into the workplace, you have to deal with any sensory problems you might have that could cause you trouble. There are a number of ways to do that as discussed in this chapter. Before you go to work, learn the social rules of the work world well by practicing them at home with your family. That is very important, for the workplace is a social institution. Learn as many organizational skills as you can as a young person because you will need them at work. Spend some time learning the ways of the work world and the ways you can do your best at work.

CHAPTER 3

Rules for Success on the Job

For my work as a livestock facilities designer, I get to travel around a lot and visit many different workplaces. Over the years, I have started to notice those qualities that make a workplace more open to people on the autism spectrum. Sometimes I even find people in workplaces, who, I think, might be on the spectrum. These people are successfully employed and many of them know nothing about autism.

Some of the jobs in which I believe I have observed undiagnosed people on the spectrum include math teacher, copier repair technician, research scientist, industrial equipment drafter, welder, factory maintenance staff, librarian, computer programmer, computer tech support and engineer. Keep these in mind when we later look at jobs that appear best suited for the strengths of individuals on the autism spectrum.

One of the most interesting workplaces I have visited is a small electronics and machine tool firm where the employees are downright passionate about their work. On my visit, each designer stopped me on my way through the workroom to show me what he was doing on his computer. I noticed that, although they worked in a room together, their workstations allowed them some distance from each other. I also noticed that the overhead fluorescent lights had been dismantled and that each workstation had its own soft lighting—all subtle signs that the employees' sensory sensitivities had been accommodated.

Whether you work for a small entrepreneurial firm or a large organization, you will still have to live up to your employer's expectations. We need to work where our talents are respected and our colleagues are tolerant of our social eccentricities.

Out in the machine shop, I got the same treatment as each guy showed off his machine and walked me through all its capabilities. Where did the employer get such passionate and interested staff members, I asked? Their supervisor told me that the company hired on talent alone and that one of the "techies" had done the interviewing. At least on the machine tool side, the staff members all came from the local community college's machining program.

While I can only suspect that some of the guys were on the autism spectrum, I know that they work in a place that would be ideal for people on the spectrum. Because the company concentrated on hiring the most talented individuals, it worried less about social skills and fitting in, usually a major concern for employers. And they allowed new staff to be hired by one of their own—a technology wizard who looked for the same kind of skill and interest in those he interviewed. New staff also skipped the human resources department, where they might have gotten stuck. This little firm was truly an oasis for those of us on the autism spectrum. Yet, these people knew nothing about autism.

But despite such positives, there can be downsides to working for small firms. Larger organizations may have more opportunities for training and promotions. In a recession, they may have more financial reserves, so there might be less chance of losing your job due to the poor economy. Also, they generally have better policies and procedures in place for protecting workers' rights.

Whether you work for a small, entrepreneurial firm or a large organization, you will still have to live up to your employer's expectations. And, if you are self-employed, you will have to meet your clients' and customers' expectations.

That is what this chapter is about. It is a guide to being successful on the job, no matter what kind of job you have, big or small. Parents have a lot to do with preparing their children for success in life, but this chapter goes into the workplace itself and discusses the dos and don'ts of surviving there.

In a way, that little electronics firm I mentioned above is the ideal to which we should aspire. We need to work where our talents are respected and our colleagues are tolerant of our social eccentricities. For as hard as we try, those of us on the autism spectrum will never be entirely "socially normal." We will not be able to easily blend with others, so we have to become so good at what we do that employers can't afford to let us go. That means you have to know what your talent is early on and then build on it. First, this is not an ideal world, either economically or socially, so you must be prepared as much as possible for layoffs or even firings. One way to do that is to develop a rapport with others in your business or industry by not only doing top-notch work, but also by attending professional and trade association meetings. I realize that might be easier said than done, but it is a step that might be critical to your livelihood. A goodly percentage of jobs are passed on through word of mouth, so you have to be around others in your profession to hear of them.

Another solution is to be prepared to freelance, to work for yourself. Many professions such as graphic arts design, computer repair, bookkeeping and others can be done successfully by freelancing. Chapter 8 is devoted to entrepreneurship.

Second, it is important to parlay your skills and talents to industries that are staying put, not transferring their plants, offices, or functions overseas. To know which industries are most stable, you must keep up with the social and economic trends that are shaping our now-global economy. That is very important for anyone in today's workplace, but especially important for those of us considered more "dispensable" to the success of the business.

I realize this may sound like a tall order, given our global and very mobile economy. It's best to look at industries and professions that are here to stay, that don't benefit by moving away. Look at the basics in life, those jobs that take care of our daily needs—food, housing, transportation and schooling, to name a few. Look at the food industry and all its related businesses—equipment manufacturers, installers, and technicians. Then there are the repair jobs, the mechanics who fix our cars, airplanes, computers, plumbing, and electrical systems. There are the maintenance staff who repair assembly lines, the tellers who count out your money at the bank, the technician who maintains the school's heating and cooling systems, and the clerk who tracks the library's book collection.

To keep up with the general economy is fairly simple:

Regularly read your local newspaper's business section to find out local as well as global news. At the public library, you'll be able to find a host of newspapers and business publications as well as trade and professional journals. Read them weekly, so you know what is going on and what to expect. Search the Internet to learn about interesting careers, some of which you may never have thought of. To know which industries are most stable, you must keep up with the social and economic trends that are shaping our current global economy.

Guidance counselors should encourage parents who work in different careers to donate trade magazines to the school library. Every profession has its professional or trade magazines, ranging from banking to car washes to building construction. These magazines will enable you to learn about all types of interesting jobs.

For a detailed look at the economy, check out the following:

The Wall Street Journal

My father subscribed me to this wonderful, in-depth, five-day-a-week business newspaper when I was a teenager. I still read it religiously to keep up with general business news as well as my own industry's news, but also to learn more about social protocol, networking, office behaviors, and other social rules that do not come easy for me. I strongly recommend that both guidance counselors and students in high school subscribe to *The Wall Street Journal.*

The Occupational Outlook Handbook

This very thick reference comes out of the United States Department of Labor every two years and includes key information on specific professions as well as a wonderful description of the economy as a whole. You can access this in both book form and the online version to check how your particular profession is faring (www.bls.gov/oco/).

Fortune Magazine, Fortune Small Business Magazine and Business Week

Every year this business publication produces its "100 Best Companies to Work For" issue, which is a great source of information about the companies workers value most. This beginning-of-the-year issue usually describes the winning companies' corporate cultures, an excellent barometer of how employers view and respect their staff members. If a company is on this list, you can bet it is more tolerant of social eccentricities.

Inc.

This in-depth publication chronicles in great detail news and information about small, entrepreneurial businesses, which provide much of the employment in the United States. Often the more entrepreneurial a company is, the more it values talent and the less it worries about social conformity.

Business Week Magazine

This publication does a good job of explaining the economy and the business world in plain, understandable language. You can find it on the newsstands, in the library periodical section or through subscription.

Trade Magazines

Read trade magazines from different industries, many of which can be accessed on the Internet.

Trade Shows

Visit conventions and trade shows to talk with people working in the field and learn about trends that way. While in Chicago recently, I visited the food industry's annual convention and saw all the interesting and new equipment for that field.

There are more, of course, but these are a good start on building a regular reading list. Information and talent are essentials to being employed in the 21st century, but they need to be practiced regularly to keep them fit. I can't stress enough that social skills for those of us on the spectrum will never be entirely smooth, so we have to have other things going for us. We have to be realistic about what will help us lead fruitful and good lives.

Based on some 30 years of travels down the autism spectrum, I have found that those who do the best have three things going for them:

- Talent that was developed over time into skills that can be used in a career.
- Mentors who helped guide them through their often confusing teen and young adult years, and who helped them get involved in interesting careers.
- Proper medication to help manage their sensory, anxiety or depression problems. *(Note: Some individuals do not need or do not choose to use medication.)*

Often the more entrepreneurial a company is, the more it values talent and the less it worries about social conformity. The most successful work hard, are on time, constantly upgrade their skills and try hard to get along with their colleagues.

In addition, the most successful work hard, are on time, constantly upgrade their skills, and try hard to get along with their colleagues. You may not like your colleagues or agree with them, but you must be respectful of them and tolerant of their differences. In other words, you treat people the way you want to be treated.

The following seven rules are the basics for being successful on the job, no matter what the job.

Rule #1: Know your strengths and your limits.
Being successful at work is like anything else: pay careful attention to what works best for you, how you like to spend your time, and what activities make you feel particularly creative and strong. That is not all there is to it, of course, but that's a lot of it.

Work, for the most part, is a social activity, even if you work alone. Sooner or later, you're going to have to deliver your work to a client or employer, and it's best if you learn how to work with others—to a degree. It won't ever be your strength, so make sure you stay out of situations that can cause problems for you. Know your limits.

I know one man on the autism spectrum who worked successfully for five years in a laboratory until he went drinking with his colleagues one night after work. In this informal setting, he could not handle the different level and type of social interaction with people who had no clue about his autism. He became drunk, acted inappropriately, and was promptly fired because he did not know his limits.

On the other hand, when you capitalize on your strengths and avoid situations for which you are not prepared, work goes more smoothly. I started my freelance design business after working for others for a while because I could manage my environment and social interactions more effectively this way. I can keep my work relationships on a technical level, so work is less stressful and more fulfilling for me.

Rule #2: Have a plan.

There are a few other things to remember about finding a job when you are on the autism spectrum. First of all, know what you want to do and get the necessary training and education for the job. For many of us on the spectrum, that entails developing talents we are born with. The best way to do that is to work closely with family members, teachers, counselors and others involved in your life. Then match your talents to the kinds of jobs that are available in your community. Work with your high school counselor to find out more about these jobs. Go to the Autism Society of America web page (www.autism-society.org), which has great information about transitioning from the school system into the workplace. Its most important message is that having a plan in place is critical.

The local community college or vocational technical school is another resource that should be used. These schools can open the door to many satisfying careers. Some really bright students may need to be taken out of the high school social pressure cooker and enroll at a university. This will enable them to find relationships through shared interests.

College courses available over the Internet are another option. These classes are ideal for many people on the spectrum. Also, a high school student who is getting teased in school may be better off taking high school classes online and graduate that way. There are a lot of scams on the Internet, so when considering that option, always make sure that online courses are being taught by a reputable, accredited institution.

Don't stop planning when you get into the workforce. Keep up-to-date on the economy. Read your local newspaper, check the Department of Labor's *Occupational Outlook Handbook*, which is listed on the Department's web page (www.bls.gov/oco/) and is found in public libraries in the reference section. This will help you plan for your future.

Rule #3: Develop a portfolio and show your work.

I am a firm believer in keeping a portfolio of copies of your best work, performance reviews, and other documents in your home rather than, or in addition to, your place of work. I talked to one person who lost a drafting design job. He had kept none of his engineering drawings to show to potential new employers. The only thing he had was an old unplayable disc for an obsolete computer system.

Print out paper copies of your best writing, drawings, PowerPoint presentations, computer programs, and other work. Keep copies of all performance reviews and letters that are complimentary. If possible, have electronic copies on hand so you can e-mail your portfolio.

Table 3.1: How to Make a Successful Portfolio

Many things can go into your portfolio, which should be gathered in an attractive notebook or folder. You can include:

- Color prints of graphic arts, work or web pages
- Copies of architectural and engineering drawings
- Copies of articles written in newspapers, magazines or newsletters
- Letters of reference
- Printouts of computer programs, spreadsheets or other work
- Photos of artwork or things you have built
- Scientific journal articles
- List of satisfied clients with references
- A résumé with information on projects that you have completed
- Photos of products you have made, such as jewelry or woodworking
- Copies of papers you have translated—include both the original language and the translation

When I first started my livestock design facilities business, I could get few others in that industry to take me seriously. What the engineers and designers saw was a woman (bad enough) with odd, off-putting mannerisms trying to talk with them about her ideas. They would only talk with me and take me seriously after I showed them my portfolio, a collection of drawings and designs.

"You drew these?" they asked skeptically. With a portfolio in hand, I could get their attention and eventually land some design jobs for my fledgling business. It was not easy and, at times, the process was downright rude and hateful. But I am here because I stuck it out and kept developing my design talent.

If you are in a field where showing your work isn't possible, you have to demonstrate what you are capable of doing in other ways. Sometimes you can show what you are capable of doing in volunteer jobs. Try working with someone you know in his or her business, just helping out in small ways at first. Volunteer at your church, synagogue, temple—all of the activities you take on when you are young can be used on your resume when you are older and job searching. Then your portfolio becomes your cover letter in which you explain and describe your concrete contributions to an organization.

Many people make the mistake of putting too much stuff in the portfolio. Pick out the best work. Five to 10 items are usually enough. Sometimes it is a good idea to have another person select your best work; this ensures more objectivity. Weird science fiction art is not the best thing to show an advertising agency that is hiring you to do car and bank ads. However, it would be the right thing to show if you were applying for a comic book artist job. Match portfolio content to the job, and even the employer. Only bring what will fit with the job for which you are applying.

Again, be prepared to have both a paper and an electronic copy of your portfolio. In some cases, old-fashioned "snail mail" is most effective because people are afraid to open e-mail attachments that could infect their computer with viruses. Make sure your materials are presented neatly. Photos and drawings should be in a notebook in plastic sleeves. Get help from mentors, teachers, even the staff at the local printing shop may have some advice. Whatever you do, make sure it looks professional.

When you are ready to e-mail or snail-mail your portfolio, make sure you have included all the pertinent contact information. I am shocked at the number of people who contact me and fail to provide complete contact information. You have to make it easy for busy people to contact you when they look at your portfolio. If they cannot contact you in the first attempt, your portfolio—no matter how great—may get buried under other work and forgotten.

When you send your portfolio, or if you just want to contact a potential employer, mentor or advisor, be sure to remember the following:

1. Include your complete postal address.
2. Include your e-mail address and make sure it has your name in it, such as JaneDoe@msn.com. Avoid using smart aleck or silly e-mail addresses when you are sending out your portfolio or employment letters; they make you look immature and unprofessional.

3. Having strong talents is critical to your job search, so practice them consistently.
4. Be sure to list all of your phone numbers: work, home and mobile.
5. Attach your contact information to your portfolio in such a way that it does not get lost.
6. Avoid sending e-mail attachments unless the person you are contacting says it is okay. People do not open attachments from individuals they don't know.
7. Use the U.S. postal service, FedEx or UPS for sending a portfolio to someone you have not previously contacted because the recipient is more likely to open it.

Rule #4: Develop your talents, no matter what they are, for they will help you in your job search.
Having strong talents is critical to your job search, so practice them consistently. At the same time, don't forget to practice your social skills, for those are terribly important as well.

But the talent is the key. It is important to develop skills in things that other people want. Architectural drafting is a valued skill, for example, whereas playing video games is not a skill employers want unless you are super good at designing them. The video game design field is very competitive—there are probably 10 people for every video game design job.

Expect the unexpected. I got my first big client because of my sewing talent. I was wearing a western shirt I had embroidered when I met the wife of the insurance agent for a meat plant. She admired my shirt, and when I told her what I did for a living, she worked it out so I met with the plant president and presented my portfolio of designs. Of course, it was more than merely luck. By then I had been writing for *Arizona Farmer Ranchman* magazine and had been around the business for a while, so I knew the industry.

Rule #5: Be prepared to enter the job market through the back door, side door, any door but the front!
There are always more doors to enter than just the front door. This is a good rule to remember when looking for work and planning a career. Front doors to jobs are usually guarded by vigilant human resources departments, whose job is to screen applicants to fit a certain mold. People on the spectrum are often some of the first ones screened out of jobs because of their social eccentricities, lack of work experience, or gaps in their work history. You have to have a talent so strong and deep that it impresses anyone meeting you.

Since people on the autism spectrum tend to be good at one skill and not so good at others, I have concentrated this book on jobs that have a low barrier of entry. Algebra was impossible for me and foreign languages were difficult. My math disability locked me out of jobs in highly competitive fields such as veterinary medicine because I could not pass the entry exams. The veterinary medicine courses would have been fairly easy for me, but I could not get beyond the prerequisites.

While highly competitive fields such as medicine and veterinary medicine have a high barrier of entry, other jobs have a wide-open back door. For example, there are many people in the computer field or highly skilled trades who have no college degree. They were self-taught and they showed a portfolio of their work to the right person. The person who can open the back door for you may be found just about anywhere as illustrated above with the insurance agent's wife. These people may be at your church, bowling club, or living right on your block, so always be open and prepared to discuss these issues.

You have to be persistent to get in the back door. I was rebuffed many times before I found the person who would open the back door. Be persistent yet be polite. That is very important. In the food industry, for example, many eccentric and talented people got into satisfying jobs by starting out on boring jobs on the processing line. After learning many different skills, they started hanging around with the maintenance staff. When the maintenance staff saw their talent, they let them work with them. In another instance, a man who started digging ditches for fiber optic cable ended up a computer expert. During breaks, he hung around the computer people. The "back door" can work in many ways.

Consider freelance work if your talent lends itself to self-employment. Often people in design, computer programming or repair, construction, maintenance and similar fields can parlay their work into a business.

Consistency at work is highly valued, and that includes getting to work on time and showing up with a cheerful, can-do attitude.

Table 3.2: Using Computers to Teach Career Skills

Many adolescents are attracted to video games and spend an inordinate amount of time playing these games. The fast-moving animation is captivating for them and keeps them glued to the screen. The video games that are the most addictive are the shooting games with lots of rapid movement. These are the games that provide no useful skills for a career. I am not against all computer video programs. Unfortunately, most of the computer programs that enlighten and educate are expensive professional software. To use them, you would need to find a scientist, engineer, or other technical professional who would let you play with these "video games" that people use in their jobs. For example, scientists use fascinating programs for visualizing complex molecules in organic chemistry. Other programs convert flat drawings into three-dimensional virtual reality buildings that you can "walk through." Simulation software available in your local computer store can be used to motivate interest in how ecosystems work, for example.

The first step in broadening a video game obsession into employable skills is to look at what the adolescent's favorite game is. For example, a game that involves smashing cars could be associated with fixing cars. A girl who loves to play fashion model games could be encouraged to learn how to sew clothes. Or a student with drawing ability could start by drawing her favorite video game characters. Since publication of the second edition, I have talked to five or six young adults who stopped playing endless video games when they were introduced to fixing cars. They discovered that motors were more interesting than video games. Today they have good jobs, such as fixing trains.

Freelancing is not for the faint hearted, though, because you have to be able to market your product or service, manage your workflow and keep good cash flow. Some individuals on the spectrum have been successful when they partnered with another person to run and manage the business. The talented person on the spectrum then works on assignments that are brought to him or her.

In some cases, I landed a design job by showing my portfolio to a guy I met on a plane. Maybe the person who can open the back door is in front of you in the supermarket checkout line. Politely introduce yourself to the fellow shopper who has a computer company badge hanging around his neck. In the early days of my career, I always had a few of my best drawings and photos of jobs in my purse. In brief, people are impressed with talent, and demonstrating your talent can often open up the back door.

Rule #6: Get to work on time, neatly dressed and with a good attitude.

This one sounds easy, but it can be difficult for people on the spectrum. Consistency at work is highly valued, and that includes getting to work on time and showing up with a cheerful, can-do attitude. Employers know they can teach the skills required for the job to their staff members, but they don't have the time to teach attitude. So, make it easy for them and come in with a good attitude and a willingness to try different things. After all, don't you want to work around people who are cheerful and pleasant?

The good thing about attitude is that it can be taught at a fairly young age by parents, teachers and counselors. My hat is off to those caring adults who take the time to help their youngster grow up independent and with a good attitude.

These rules for success have helped me over my years in the workforce, and I think they are just as true for others as they have been for me. Working is a wonderful experience, a human experience, and one to be treasured and be grateful for. It has been the bedrock in my life.

Rule #7: Don't get involved in unethical or illegal situations in the workplace.

When people on the spectrum see an unethical or illegal situation at work, our first inclination is to try and fix it, to clean it up or make it go away. We live by the rules, and we expect others to do so, too. So when we know something is going on that is unfair, it really bothers us.

For instance, your colleague applies for a promotion and you just know she will get it because her work is excellent and her attitude positive. So when your boss' friend from another department ends up being hired for the position, you are shocked and then angered by the unfairness of it all. Although this situation is upsetting, it is probably not illegal, but it is unethical. There's a difference, and it is very important to remember; to be illegal, an action has to break a law. So if your colleague heard that she didn't get promoted to the new position because she was too old, or because of her ethnicity, that is illegal. Workplaces are not allowed to discriminate in hiring or promoting.

When we are faced with such a problem, our first inclination is to tell someone in authority because when people on the spectrum see an unethical or illegal situation at work, our first inclination is to try and fix it.

Remember that the workplace, just like everything else in this world, is not perfect. We like issues in our lives to be clear-cut and straightforward. But please consider your reactions to these problems in the workplace very carefully.

First, if you have this type of concern talk with a trusted mentor or individual, someone with a lot of professional experience but not someone from your current workplace. Be careful how you communicate though. Don't use e-mails to discuss the problem—and never send such e-mails at work—because they can be retrieved and used if the situation ends up in court.

Second, if you eventually decide to talk with someone at work, talk with the person who hired you. Don't go over your boss' head; include him or her in discussions of your concerns and decide on your course of action after a lot of hard thinking and consulting with others.

Remember that the workplace, just like everything else in this world, is not perfect and that there will be problems of one type of another. Therefore, the issue should be a very serious one before you risk becoming involved. Also, if you do report a problem at work, you can expect that you will suffer in some way yourself, whether from angry colleagues or bosses, possibly even losing your job. So when you're trying to decide what to do, consider the following questions before acting:

- How serious is the problem? Is it unethical or an actual danger to others? What will happen if you don't do anything?
- Does it involve dangerous products that could hurt employees or customers?
- Does it involve cheating low-income people or others who have fewer resources with which to protect themselves?

Those of us on the spectrum have a lot of wonderful talents and skills, but understanding and dealing with tense and unusual social situations is not one of them. It would not be wise in general for us to become whistleblowers, those employees who publicly report unscrupulous and illegal workplace activities. They often lose their jobs and are treated like traitors. The situation has to be extremely serious and hurtful to those who cannot defend themselves. Think Enron Energy Corporation, whose financial manipulations caused a lot of employees to lose their retirement money.

I can't emphasize this enough: make sure the problem is extremely serious before you get involved with it.

Conclusion

Just as in other parts of our lives, there are definite "rules" for success in the work world. For many people on the autism spectrum, these rules are particularly challenging due to their innate characteristics involving communication, emotions and social skills. Nevertheless, with proper preparation as outlined in this book, steps can be taken to ensure that one's true talents predominate—in other words, the focus here is on how to maximize your strengths. For those of us on the autism spectrum, there seem to be some general characteristics of successful individuals:

- Talent that was developed over time into skills that can be used in a career.
- Mentors who helped guide them through their confusing teen and young adult.
- Proper medication to help manage their sensory, anxiety or depression problems. *(Note: There are some individuals who do not need medication.)*

To be successful in the workplace as a person with autism spectrum disorders, please consider this advice as well:

- Know your strengths and limits
- Have a plan
- Create a portfolio of your work
- Develop your talents
- Be prepared to enter the job market through the "back" door
- Be on time and have a good attitude

Just as in other parts of our lives, there are definite "rules" for success in the work world.

CHAPTER 4

Finding a Vocation You Love

C hoosing a career or vocation is one of the most important decisions people make in their lives. Because we spend so much time working, we want a job that is a good fit for our lives. We want something we can grow into, and that matches our strengths, interests, and lives. That is why it is so important to be careful about choosing your work.

In our increasingly complex world, jobs are also growing both more complicated and broad. So it's important to figure out what you do best, what you enjoy, before even beginning a job search. This takes time, but as you are about to find out in this chapter, there are some rather pleasant and "natural" ways to discover your vocational calling.

As we have emphasized throughout the previous chapters, cultivate your talent. You do this by paying attention to your interests, recording your observations, and talking with others about your shared interests.

Parents Play a Big Role

Parents play the most important role in the task of getting youths on the autism spectrum ready for the job world. If you are the parent of a child on the autism spectrum, help your child cultivate his or her strengths early on. How?

By observing and listening and an awful lot of reflection. Notice his or her interests and passions—even if they seem a little off the wall or different. If your youngster is a whiz at taking things apart, be sure to have plenty of Legos at home. Save boxes so your daughter can build a city, grocery store or a sculpture. For older children, science project kits are recommended. If you find your son plopped down on the ground studying an ant trail, get down with him and watch those ants at work. Learn about the natural world with him; check out books from the library, spend time outdoors walking that ant trail. Be delighted if your child is attracted to something like ants. With an interest in nature, children become explorers, opening up their lives even more.

Parents should carefully expand their children's horizons by starting with their interests and talents. It is these passions that will help them navigate the world. Don't do this alone, though. Incorporate other caring adults into this community, people who will take your child places, who can talk with her about their interests, and who can even help her discover new ones.

If you're not sure about your child or student's skills or strengths, ask yourself these questions:

1. What are the child's best subjects in school, the ones in which he gets the best grades?
2. What is the child's special interest?
3. What is he really good at?

There are a lot of resources available for introducing young people on the spectrum to careers. Start early in the child's life and investigate resources such as the following:

1. Community colleges—a good place to find mentors and many career courses.
2. Online learning programs—offered by community colleges, colleges and universities on a variety of subjects
3. Technical schools that offer automotive, drafting and other industrial subjects.
4. Parents: teach your child your own profession. For example, many computer programmers enter the field as their parents' apprentice.
5. The federal government's *Occupational Outlook Handbook* (www.bls.gov/oco)—a classic reference about jobs, compiled by the U.S. Department of Labor
6. Church, synagogue, mosque and temple—find mentors in a variety of fields and industries at your family's place of worship. Be sure to show the child's portfolio of work to interested people.
7. Interesting work sites: visit construction sites, radio stations, research labs, bank computer centers,

graphic design studios and other places of interest to your child.

8. Large bookstores—good places to find books on computer programming and other fields, or just about anything.

Individuals on the spectrum often have obsessions about particular subjects that, if used properly, could propel them into a paying career. However, parents, teachers and counselors must help them make a connection between their special interests and the world of work. The autistic mind is associational, so use the motivation of the obsession to stimulate ideas about a career that can be associated with the special interest.

You can help them broaden their special interest at the same time you begin teaching them how to respond to what other people may need or want. This is an excellent way to help a young person on the spectrum prepare for the outside world of work and responsibilities to others. Here's an example of this process at work—how you would help a young man who is obsessed with drawing NASCAR racing cars broaden his interests:

Step 1. Expand first by drawing a racetrack or picture of a driver.

Step 2. Next draw a house for a driver to live in.

Step 3. Draw a food the driver would like.

Step 4. Draw your own house and favorite food.

Step 5. Draw your friends' favorite food.

Step 6. Draw houses and cars shown in a magazine that another person reads.

Individuals on the spectrum often have obsessions about particular subjects that, if used properly, could propel them into a paying career.

Gradually teach the concept of drawing work that other people will appreciate and pay for. In this example, the association with NASCAR is still there, but it becomes more and more distant.

Here are a few other examples of how to link other special interests to paying careers:

Special Interest	Link to a Career
Building with Legos	construction, architectural design, engineering, drafting, or building industrial equipment
Everything about Windows software	computer programming
Drawing cartoon characters	graphic design, fine art, industrial design, web design
Playing Mario video games	plumbing, graphic design (start by drawing pictures of Mario)
Playing car crash, crime video games	automotive mechanic (repair cars, don't crash them), forensic science (solve crimes), video games
Trains or cars	automotive mechanic, vehicle designer

Special Interest	Link to a Career
Dogs or horses	riding teacher, animal trainer, veterinary technician
Insects	entomologist, research scientist
Weather statistics	weather forecasting, record keeping
History	(common interest of autistics)—accounting (associate with how it was done in medieval times), library science (preserving history), journalism (writing about events that will become history)

These interests are a big part of your child's life, and therefore are a part of yours as well.

For myself, I loved to draw as a youngster and build things. When I was little, I built things from cardboard. Building skills learned as a child translated into building things from wood and steel as an adult. I loved using my hands to build and my visual thinking skills to design.

Thankfully, my parents had the foresight to allow me to develop those talents by signing me up for classes, buying me books, and so on, and years later, I turned them into a paying vocation.

Developing talents does not have to be expensive. Community centers, parks and recreation departments, colleges, school districts, and other organizations provide low-cost, sometimes no-cost programs to the public. They also offer sports, arts and crafts, foreign languages, summer camps and other organized activities. For adults, colleges offer continuing education courses, ranging from computer skills to robotics to horsemanship. Many 4-H centers provide horsemanship training as well as other interesting programs for children and teens.

Lobbying for Your Child:
One Parent's Success Story

As a parent support supervisor at a community mental health center, Tanya Parsons works with families of children with special needs. Her advice is especially valuable to these parents because she too has raised a child with special needs—now 25 years old, employed and living on his own. Years ago, Parson's son, James, was diagnosed with major depression, sensory system problems and dyslexia. If he was being diagnosed today, James' doctor has said, he would probably be diagnosed as having autism.

Helping James grow up has not been easy for Parsons, a single parent of two. "It's been important to me to help both my children put down roots and live stable lives," she says.

This is the story of how she has helped her son do just that.

I always tell parents that they are their child's best advocates once they find their voice. When they begin meeting with all the various people and agencies that can help their child, they need to ask for more than they think they can have. You would be surprised at how well that can work for the child. But parents also need to be diplomatic and polite, thank people for their help and show appreciation for what they have done to help their family.

I also tell parents to get the notes from these meetings right away, to have the counselor or staff person they met with immediately photocopy their notes from the meeting, so parents can leave with them. This way you know exactly what was said and what was agreed would be done.

I want parents to be thinking about their child's future. Just last week I was telling a group of parents that it is important to know not just how to use the system for their children, but how to use it to help their children be independent.

When James was about to graduate from high school, I discontinued his IEP and switched him to a 504 accommodations plan to help him make the transition to college. I did this primarily because colleges don't offer IEPs, but they do make accommodations plans for students with disabilities. James had won a four-year scholarship to the San Francisco Art Institute, and I did a lot before he left for school to make the transition smoother. I flew out to meet with his instructors, arranged for a psychologist to work with him and hired a tutor, which Vocational Rehabilitation paid for. I basically went out there and set up a wrap-around team for him. James signed the release of information form, so I was able to talk regularly with his instructors and the art institute staff. Our baseline was that James would show up for class, whether he had done his homework or not.

I really had my nose in his business. Altogether, I believe I made about six or seven trips out there, setting up his wrap-around team and visiting. The art institute didn't have dorms, so James lived in an apartment. Over time he became more depressed. Finally, my daughter and I had to move him back home because he had disintegrated so much. When he got home, all he could do was lie on the couch, which scared me terribly. It was so much like his first major episode of depression that I felt we were going to have to start all over again.

Everyone had advice for me, most of it the same—to get James up off the couch and get busy with something. But I felt he needed to rest, that his experience at school had taken a lot out of him. So I let him be and just waited for him to come around, and after three months he did.

This approach might not work for everyone, but I think you have to follow your own instincts with your children. All along I had kept close contact with James' vocational rehabilitation counselor, asking that his case be kept open until James could come up with something, a job, he wanted to do. It's important for parents with special needs kids to bond with the people who are helping their child and to always keep them in the loop.

Well, after about three months of rest, James told me he wanted to become a bike mechanic, and we did some research about training programs. vocational rehabilitation paid for the training, and now James works as a bike mechanic 20 hours a week. He can't work full time because he becomes overly fatigued, so he still receives

Social Security Disability Insurance to supplement his income and health care benefits through the state.

James continued to live with me for a while, but one day his sister dropped by, upset because her roommates were moving out and she would have to move out of her house. Surprisingly, James volunteered to move in with her to help her meet expenses. I held my breath because his sister had helped take care of him so much while he was young, but it turned out to be a wonderful transition to independent living for him. Later he lived in a house with a bunch of other young people, which was a good experience for him, too. Now he owns a home through the city's Tenants to Homeowners program, and lives just a couple blocks away from me. James has a good life, with friends, interests and a job he likes.

Raising a child with these kinds of needs means there are a lot of ups and downs in life. I know I am now much kinder to myself than ever before. I warn the parents I work with not to become isolated. I tell them to join a support group, to have a friend they can tell things to. It took me a long time to join a support group, and for the first few meetings I just sat on the edge of the group and cried. Now I facilitate that very same group.

I think it is pretty common for families of children with special needs to suffer from post-traumatic stress syndrome, just from all the ups and downs of raising their children. They need to care for themselves, too.

(Tanya and James Parsons are pseudonyms used to protect the family's privacy.)

Cultivating Your Talents

I can't emphasize enough that people with autism must be extremely talented in their vocation to make up for challenges in social skills. They have to be so good at what they do that people will want to buy their skills. They have to be so good at what they do that they are the last ones laid off during a recession because the employer does not want to lose their talents to someone else.

This is why parents have to start young with their children, supporting them in building their talents, teaching them about the world, and helping them navigate that world as best they can. That is why making a portfolio of your work—even as a youngster—is so important to the job search process. Start early. The more proof you have of your capabilities, the better off you will be in the workplace. And the more choices of places to work you will have.

Working with Your Child's School

Schools can be another resource for parents of children on the autism spectrum. If your son loves to draw, make sure the art teacher knows that. If music moves your daughter, tell that to the school music teacher. Early on, build relationships with the teachers whose expertise and interest match your child's. Do not leave out your child's classroom teacher. He or she can be a valuable resource for helping your child do well and thrive in school.

Schools sometimes focus on the deficits in students' lives, and not their abilities. That is a major mistake.

Instead, schools must focus on helping students build on their strengths and work toward goals that will help them become successful. There are many talented individuals on the autism spectrum, but somehow along the way, often their talents were not cultivated and therefore did not flourish into paying jobs. That is a terrible waste.

Parents of children on the autism spectrum must keep an open, flexible mind about their children's abilities and motivations. Allow your children to spend time developing their fixations into hobbies. Encourage them in any way you can, for that will help.

Taking Advantage of Vocational Rehabilitation Services

But don't do this alone, parents. Enroll your child in your state's Vocational Rehabilitation (VR) program transition services, designed to help individuals with disabilities prepare for the workforce and independence. VR offers services for eligible high school juniors and seniors to help them transition from school to their communities, including the following:

- Assessment/vocational evaluation
- Transition services at Community Rehabilitation Programs
- Career guidance and counseling

- On-the-job training (OJT)
- Cooperative Work-Experience Program (COOP)
- Assistance with job-seeking skills
- Assistance with finding a job
- Supported employment job coaching
- Sheltered employment certification
- Personal/vocational adjustment training and/or college preparation training
- Assistive technology device/service

If your high school junior or senior has a VR plan, he or she can get work experience and credits through COOP. It is one of several transition services provided by VR in partnership with individual school districts. Being involved in high school VR programs can save you a lot of grief when your son or daughter graduates and loses the support the high school provided. VR fills that gap as it helps your youngster ease into independence.

That transition will proceed more smoothly if the VR counselor is part of the student's IEP team, advises Greg Hill, a senior counselor in the Missouri Division of Vocational Rehabilitation. The counselor can help plan the student's transition into college, job training or the workforce. After graduation, students transfer into the adult VR program, where they make an Individualized Plan for VR offers services for eligible high school juniors and seniors to help them transition from school to their communities.

Employment (IPE) with a Counselor

The IPE includes a long-range vocational goal and the kind of assistance needed. In addition to the VR Transition Program services, this arm of VR also offers:

- Individual counseling during the rehabilitation process
- Vocational training to prepare for employment, including tuition/fees, books and supplies for education in a college, university, trade school, community rehabilitation program or on-the-job training program
- Basic living and transportation costs necessary for participation in a training program
- Job-related tools and licenses when the client is ready to go to work
- Medical, surgical, psychiatric or hospital care to reduce or remove disabling conditions that could prevent the client from working

There is no one profession that is best for people with disabilities, Hill says. It's more important to develop strong relationships with individual employers. For some, entrepreneurship is a vocational goal, and VR funds small business training. More information on entrepreneurship for people on the spectrum is discussed in Chapter 8.

Another tool for achieving independence, Hill says, is the Social Security Administration's Plan for Achieving Self- Support (PASS). Although somewhat complicated, developing a PASS plan can be worth the trouble because it can help support the vocational and small business goals of those receiving Social Security benefits. Basically, having a PASS plan means any extra income individuals make won't be counted against their benefits and can be used toward vocational goals.

Since the plan is complex, getting help in writing it is important, advises Tim McElvoy, a PASS coordinator for Social Security. VR counselors can help, and so can the local Social Security Work Incentives Planning Assistance office. The goal is to find a vocation that pays well enough, so that SSI benefits can eventually be reduced or eliminated.

Some might use the income to purchase supplies or equipment for their start-up business. Others may decide to enroll in a trade school to learn a new skill. But whatever the long-range goal, PASS allows people to set aside money to pay for expenses, including:

- Transportation to and from work
- Tuition, books, fees and supplies needed for school or training
- Childcare
- Attendant care
- Employment services, such as job coaching and resumé writing
- Supplies to start a business
- Equipment and tools to do the job
- Uniforms, special clothing and safety equipment

DEVELOPING TALENTS

Mentoring

For many children and teenagers on the autism spectrum, schools are not always the friendliest places. Often, autistic teens misbehave in school because they get bored. So it's especially important to help your child find a mentor in his interest area to keep him learning and plugged into life.

I was lucky to have a wonderful high school science teacher, Mr. Carlock, who taught me how to do scientific research, a skill I have used repeatedly in my career and personal life. His mentoring helped steer me into a career that has combined my scientific and design interests. Mr. Carlock, like all good mentors, also encouraged me when the trials and tribulations of high school wore me down. Like others on the autism spectrum, I hyper-focused on pet subjects, which drove my fellow high school students and administrators nuts. The teasing was terrible, but Mr. Carlock's kindness and encouragement helped me get through and channeled those fixations into something larger than just myself—a vocation.

As I stated earlier, I was a poor student. The only subject I did well in was biology; I had no motivation to study English or history. Algebra was an incomprehensible mystery to me. My motivation in school improved when I realized that I had to study in order to be able to do the things I wanted to do. A good mentor can build motivation for schoolwork by using the motivation behind fixations.

The one mistake that was made in my education was a futile attempt to learn algebra. I was never allowed to try trigonometry or geometry. I could have learned these with hands-on projects such as building a model bridge.

Over the years, I have talked with a lot of parents and successful people on the spectrum about what has worked for them and their children, and I am convinced that the beginning of most successful careers involves mentors. To get career interests started, the child received some formal instruction from their parents, a friend or a teacher. This "teaching" is essential to develop innate abilities and "light the fuse" that gets a career launched. In the computer industry, a career home for many on the spectrum, some of the most successful careers began with some formal instruction from mentors. Below are some examples of how mentoring started successful careers:

1. A mother teaches her son an old computer language that she used when she first started out. This sparked an interest in programming, and her son went on to learn modern computer languages on his own. He ended up in a successful programming career.

2. My high school science teacher, Mr. Carlock, motivated me to become interested in science, but he also taught me critical skills such as how to research scientific journal articles.

3. A successful video photographer learned photography from a family friend as a child.

4. John Elder Robison, author of *Look Me in the Eye: My Life with Asperger's*, was mentored as teenager by a university professor who let him visit the university science labs.

A mentor is one of the best kinds of help for those searching for a vocation. In a way, a mentor is a must for adults and teenagers on the autism spectrum because he or she can help them use their fixations in a positive way. Those fixations, researcher Leo Kanner (1971) notes, provide great motivation and can lead to careers and even a social life. Mentors help students discover and develop their talents, coach them in their decision-making and help them stay on task.

Schools and some workplaces offer mentorship programs, but mentors can be found just about anywhere. As mentioned, I found one of my first meat industry mentors when I met the wife of his insurance agent at a party. She liked my hand-embroidered western shirt, on which I had spent hours embroidering a steer head, and later helped me make the right connections.

Discover Your Strengths

There are other ways of discovering your strengths, and ultimately mentors as well. Author Richard Nelson Bolles suggests in *What Color Is Your Parachute?* (2003) that job seekers should study other people's lives and then ask themselves, "Now, whose job would I most like to have?"

Author Marsha Sinetar (1987) writes that adults seeking a career should leave enough time to discover their "right livelihood." Ideally, that should begin in childhood, but if it doesn't, there is still time. Start, Sinetar suggests, by noticing what you like, how you like spending your time, what activities give you energy—feed your soul in a way. Notice what individuals you pay attention to and what strikes you about them. Seek out role models and study their lives.

Table 4.1: Your Dream Job

To get started, try the following exercise.

1. Make a list of your first choices of jobs.
2. List your second and third choices as well.
3. List their job characteristics on separate pieces of paper.
4. Examine the lists and select the job that most interests you.
5. Find someone doing that job. Visit with him or her to find out more about the job, ask about likes and dislikes and take notes.
6. Get more ideas by studying everyone you know, have seen on TV or read about in newspapers. And take notes, so you can understand the information more thoroughly.

Study the lives of unique people to discover how they found their vocation, their work. Read biographies of people you admire. Many famous musicians and scientists were probably on the autism spectrum. How did they find their vocation? What steps did they take to make sure they were successful? Pay particular attention to how they found themselves. What values are important to them and how do they express them in their daily lives?

In the meantime, write about what you are noticing, both about the outside world and your own inner world. Keep a journal because by tracking your thoughts, you will discover your vocation in a timely—and interesting—fashion.

Visit Interesting Workplaces

People with autism may get highly motivated if they visit a workplace that sparks their interest. If that is not possible, read the trade magazines from different industries or visit a trade show. Recently, I went to the Food Expo at McCormick Place Convention Center in Chicago and saw amazing machines that make ice cream novelties. As I walked through the show, I thought somebody had to invent these machines, and it is likely some of the inventors are on the spectrum. The Food Expo would be a great place to take a high schooler who was bored with school. There are things in the world that are more interesting than video games.

Conclusion

Finding a vocation you love is very important to your well-being. The process itself can also be very enjoyable. You'll learn a lot about yourself, about what's important to you and to your family. While in the midst of it, keep these points in mind:

- Cultivate your talent by practicing it as often as you can, whether it is art, chess, music, or writing. Parents, help your children find their talents early on in life.
- Be as talented as you can in your interest or chosen field, for that is the best way to find and keep a job you love.
- Study or observe people whose jobs interest you. Visit with them about their jobs and make sure to keep notes of your conversations and observations.
- Visit interesting workplaces, so you can learn more about the world of work.

In the next chapter, you'll find information about a job search process that is just as rewarding as the job you end up finding.

CHAPTER 5

Searching for an Ideal Job

I landed my first professional job while I was still in graduate school. It happened like this: At a rodeo I walked up to the publisher of the *Arizona Farmer Ranchman Magazine* and asked if he would be interested in an article on squeeze chutes design. He was, so I wrote it up—"The Great Headgate Controversy"—and sent it off to him the very next week. The magazine published it, and I had my first job in the livestock industry.

I was still writing my thesis when all this happened, so freelancing was a great way for me to find out more about my chosen industry. I made a lot of contacts, learned more about the business of livestock facilities design, and figured out how to get my foot in the door. Publishing eventually led me to a job designing cattle chutes at a large feedlot construction company. Would I have gotten that job if I had not first worked as a freelance writer? Maybe, but it would have taken a lot longer, I bet. The contacts I made as a freelance writer allowed me to get to know the industry in a way I couldn't have as just a graduate student working on her thesis.

My point is that you have to get out and talk with people to discover the best jobs for yourself. In addition to researching and reading about careers, you have to spend some time visiting with people, asking them about their work in order to find out as much about careers and jobs as possible. That is what this chapter is about—the actual job search process. Even if you don't know your talents yet or what your career interests are, you can still follow this tried-and-true approach to finding the job for which you are best suited.

There are many ways to plan a career and find a job, but the process always starts with knowing your strengths and then identifying the job you want that fits those strengths. Chapter 4 discussed the ways to look for those career-building skills and abilities—your talents—and this chapter takes it one step further, to the job search process.

Know Yourself

The job search process can be confusing, but it can be pretty exciting. Not only are you seeking meaningful work, you are also getting to know more about yourself, what's important—and not important—for your life. That in itself is a great gift and great information to have.

Start by reflecting on what you already know about your interests and strengths. What brings you fulfillment? What piques your curiosity and energizes you so you want to jump out of bed each morning ready to start the day? I realize that these questions may sound odd in the context of the job search process. But once again, since we spend so much time working, we might as well make it enjoyable and fulfilling. Especially for those of us on the autism spectrum, having the right job can add such depth and beauty to our lives that is more than worth the effort it takes to figure out what will be the right livelihood for us.

To discover these more "hidden" elements of our lives, we sometimes need a spark to get us thinking. We can ask ourselves the questions, but we often need some outside help in understanding what's important. This outside help can take many forms, all the way from personality/traits questionnaires to sophisticated software programs found at college career centers, for example. These tools can provide a lot of good information, but ultimately they are just reflections of who you are. And after you take them, it is still up to you to use the information in such a way that it helps you determine your course of action.

If possible, visit different workplaces such as a research lab, architectural firm or construction company. There are probably many people at your church or school who could arrange a tour. Also, look at the trade magazines of different industries you think you may be interested in.

Table 5.1: Coming to Grips with What You Would Like in a Job

Start by asking yourself a series of questions about how you like to spend your time, your day, your work time.

- What does your perfect job look like?
- What does your ideal day look like?
- To find out, brainstorm a checklist of your job criteria.
- What do you need in your ideal job?
- Is variety important to you, or would you rather have the same tasks each day?
- Would you rather work in a more structured environment, or is an informal, somewhat free-flowing schedule better for you?
- Do you prefer to work alone or with others?
- Do you want to manage projects?
- Think about what is negotiable and not negotiable about your job.
- How much money do you need to make to pay your bills, and support yourself?
- Are your hours negotiable?
- Are you able to travel for work?

Job criteria. To make the criteria in Table 5.1 as concrete as possible, write them out in complete sentences. Doing that will help you have a better understanding of what's important to you in a job. For example, you have decided you like to work with other people on projects, but you also need to work a fair amount of time by yourself.

You could state that as: I want to work in a team atmosphere, but definitely need to have my own office or work part of the time from home.

If you know you are good at planning projects, you might say something like this: I want to be in charge of creating and organizing projects that solve specific problems for clients and the organization.

While writing down the criteria will help you focus on what's important to you in a job, writing down the statements in complete sentences helps you with the beginnings of a job description. Having that description makes the job search a hundred times easier and more fruitful. A surprising part of this exercise is that once you have stated what you want in a job, synchronicity sets in. In synchronicity, your stated intentions attract people and opportunities to you that will help move along your job search. But that can't happen until you've made those intentions concrete by writing them down.

In other words, writing down what you want and need in a job makes it more likely you will be able to find that particular job.

Once you have brainstormed these qualities, organize them by their importance as follows:

- What must you have in your job?
- What would you like to have?
- What is negotiable?

Once you know what's most important in a job—the criteria you have established—you are ready to look at the job skills and abilities you possess that will help you land a job.

One added benefit of this kind of focusing effort is the psychological effect. It is calming, and that is usually desperately needed during a job search. By having a written checklist and job description, you are less likely to become stuck in the sometimes grinding despair that can go along with a job hunt. It feels good to have something concrete to work with. For instance, in any job I would do, I would have to be able to use my visual design skills. In addition, I would like to have a flexible schedule since I am also teaching at a college. Finally, travel is negotiable for me.

Features and Benefits

Once you have figured out what you want and need in a job, you are ready to catalog the feature you have to offer.

Features refer to those skills, expertise, abilities and traits, credentials and work style you have to offer. The following exercise helps you identify the positive abilities you bring to a job. Also, by discovering these skills for yourself, you are in a better position to explain to employers or clients how you can benefit them.

Start by thinking of your core traits. Are you persistent, focused, attentive to details, and time conscious? Are you able to think through situations and come up with a plan to solve a problem? In the skills department, do you draw well, write well, work well with others? Are you creative, good with money, able to work alone and complete projects?

Now take those traits and skills—those specific abilities and expertise you have developed such as effective writing, instruction, or maintenance—and turn them into benefits, that is, the positive impact you can create for an employer, or clients if you are self-employed.

In a job interview or sales proposal, understanding how you can benefit someone's job, project or organization is very important. For instance, if you have determined one of your strengths is strong writing skills, you could say you would be able to save an organization time in preparing reports. Similarly, if you are particularly adept at problem solving, the benefit would be that you can smoothly move projects along and keep the workflow on an even keel. It is these kinds of benefits that will help you land the right job. It is the benefits that employers and clients are interested in—they are the concrete proof of your abilities and skills.

In summary, my most unique feature and its benefit would be the ability to quickly analyze a classroom situation and help the teacher find a workable solution, saving the college the expense and hassle of having to hire a new instructor and ensuring students receive the education they deserve and need.

DEVELOPING TALENTS

**Table 5.2: Inventory of My Features and Benefits
to Potential Employers/Clients**

My Features

1. _____

2. _____

3. _____

4. _____

5. _____

6. _____

Benefits of My Features to Future Employer/Clients

1. _____

2. _____

3. _____

4. _____

5. _____

6. _____

Adapted by permission from J. Benjamin, B. Stanny, & K. Duffy. (1995).
How to Be Happily Employed in Kansas City. *Kansas City, Missouri:
Career Management Press, p. 20.*

**Table 5.3: Sample Inventory of My Features and Benefits
to Potential Employers/Clients**

My Features

- 16 years' experience in teaching
- Strong writing skills
- Able to balance several projects at the same time
- Good at helping students and others understand new concepts
- Effective time management skills
- 8 years of mentoring experience

My Benefits

- Can develop and teach a wide variety of classes
- Am able to quickly analyze and address students' learning needs
- Can step into a new teacher's classroom, analyze the situation and collaborate on solutions
- Can produce effective reports and articles on a variety of subjects

---

"30-Second Commercial"

Never go to a job interview unless you have developed a list of benefits and are able to articulate them. To do so, try practicing a "30-second commercial" before you talk with potential employers. This exercise helps you focus on your strengths, and at the same time it gives you the confidence and self-assurance you need to get through what many people feel is one of the toughest situations they have to face. Arm yourself with this exercise and it will make your interview will go much better.

Prepare and then practice this exercise until you can get your crucial information to 30 seconds. Shortness is key here, because employers, actually all of us, size up people we meet very quickly. So in a job interview, it is particularly important to get your message across as quickly as possible, and as polished as possible. You want to go into job interviews sounding poised and sure of your abilities—and, most important, how those abilities will help the company you are approaching.

Table 5.4: How to Create a "30-Second Commercial"

1. Determine what skills you want to use on the job: writing, drawing, planning.
2. Decide what job function you want to perform: sales, design, management, teaching, and programming.
3. List your strong interests or preferences: software design, program planning.
4. Define the kinds of problems you want to solve on the job: maintaining good communication flow with clients or employees; organizing new data for projects.
5. Describe the type of results you want to produce: creating improved databases for clients, designing effective web pages, maintaining heating and cooling equipment.

6. Describe the kind of environment you want to work in: use your job criteria list on (see pages 63-64). Do you like highly structured workplaces or do you work better in an informal environment with more autonomy?

7. Finish the following thought: "I know I can do this because I have (cite specific work examples that highlight your features)."

8. List the direct results (benefits) of the above statement.

9. Practice your commercial and have someone videotape you, so you can perfect it.

Adapted by permission from J. Benjamin, B. Stanny, & K. Duffy. (1995).
How to Be Happily Employed in Kansas City. *Kansas City, Missouri:*
Career Management Press, p. 23.

Get to Know Your Community

When planning a career, you have to know your "community," both the geographic and career communities. By getting to know the kind of jobs that are available in your area, profession, or field, you will have a much better chance of landing the kind of job you want. One of the best ways to do that is also one of the most enjoyable—informal interviewing.

Informal interviewing/brainstorming. In this kind of interview, you are simply finding out about different jobs in order to match your skills to a job description. You are ready for this step because you now know what's important in a job for you, and how your skills could benefit an employer or client. You may not know what job titles fit the kind of skills you possess, but you can find out simply by talking with others about their jobs.

If talking with others is difficult for you, start practicing now. Make a point of talking with a new person each day not necessarily about your job search—but about other interests. Talk to people who actually do the work instead of the human resources department. Find out what being an artist, a librarian, or a programmer is really like. Many people you could interview would be people you see every day in your community. In the beginning, it is easier to start with people you already know. This kind of practice will prepare you for talking with others about your job search. Get as much practice as you need before you start talking about careers. But don't get so caught up in practicing that you can't get out the door to put it to work. Give yourself a deadline for getting started and have a trusted friend or family member "coach" you out the door.

Table 5.5: Example of "30-Second Commercial"

Outline

1. Three skills I want to use are planning, writing, and coaching.
2. The job function I want to perform is training.
3. My strong interests are course design and training.
4. The kinds of problems I want to solve are related to classroom instruction.

---

5. The type of results I want to produce are getting more teachers to use active learning and learner-focused curricula in their classes so students leave the college with an excellent education and a lifelong interest in learning.

6. The type of environment I want to work in is flexible and collaborative.

Final Version

I'm looking for a training position in a community college or other educational organization where my 16 years of planning, writing and training can make a difference in the quality of education students receive and the quality of teaching instructors provide.

I like working in a flexible environment where I have a lot of variety in my duties and can collaborate with my colleagues in developing student-focused curricula and programs that address how students learn most effectively.

In my past position as faculty mentor, I was responsible for training all new adjunct faculty through one-on-one mentoring sessions and regular professional development seminars that I developed, marketed and facilitated. For this job, I collaborated with faculty from all six divisions and conducted planning sessions with college Instructional and Student Services administrators.

By taking this very important step in career planning, you are not only finding out valuable information about careers in your community, you are also expanding your network of people who know you are looking for a career. In a sense, you are building a team of people interested in your job search, who are keeping their ears to the ground about job leads for you.

You are also creating your own personal database of job characteristics. By expanding your knowledge of the kind of jobs that are available in your community, you are making your own job search much easier. Start this step by making a list of everyone you know, friends, family, neighbors, and colleagues. This will speed up the job search process immensely because most jobs are found through people we know whether casually or closely.

Even if you have already worked in one field, keep an open mind to others. Just because you worked as a mechanic does not mean you have to continue working as a mechanic, but you should stay in a field that would use a mechanic's visual thinking skills if that's your special talent. For example, accounting would not usually be an appropriate switch for a mechanic. By keeping your mind open to other careers where your skills and abilities would be valued, you are expanding your job horizons. This is critical in our rapidly changing economy where people must keep up their skills in order to stay in the job market.

Table 5.6: List of Useful Contacts for My Job Search

Name	Address	Phone/Email	Job Title	Relationship

Even if you have already worked in one field, keep an open mind to others.

By conducting informal interviews, you will also get feedback on your presentation without it coming from a stranger, and you will get additional ideas about your goals, and often some pretty good advice on how to achieve them. To top it off, you will get names of people working in jobs that are interesting to you.

To prepare for an informal interview, it is often a good idea to have business cards and stationery letterhead printed. This is not necessary, or even appropriate, for every job, but if you are applying for a white-collar or professional job, that attention to detail will give the interview a more professional touch and also help you take on a job seeker's persona.

Write out a list of five questions to ask during the interview. You may end up asking more than five, but these will be your core questions.

When you contact your interviewees, ask if they would like you to send the questions to them ahead of time. Some people appreciate the extra time to think about an interview, so you are doing them a service—and, of course, you, too, are benefiting by preparing ahead of time. Try to get your interviews completed in about 30 minutes and let the interviewees know that is the timeframe you are aiming for. If it goes longer at the interviewee's request, that is fine—but it must be his or her decision.

For the interview itself, dress as you would for a regular job interview—neatly and conservatively. Find out from someone working in the same field how dressed up you have to be. For instance, if you are interested in auto repair, do you have to wear a suit and tie to the informal interview? Probably not. Each profession has its own dress code, and you want to dress within the code—and always neatly.

Table 5.7: Questions to Ask During Informal Interviews

1. How would you describe your job?
2. How long have you been working in the field?
3. What kinds of changes in your field have you seen occur since you started, and what do you predict will happen over the next few years?
4. What's the best and worst attributes of your field?
5. What skills and abilities are important for your field?

Be on time and start the interview by thanking the person for spending the time with you, even if it is a close family member. This is good manners and is an important part of workplace culture. If this is your first job, it gets you in the practice of being in the workplace.

During the interview, make as much eye contact as you can and listen actively to the person with whom you are talking. Do not interrupt, but feel free to ask additional questions if the person talks about a topic that is interesting to you and concerns your job search. The latter is important. You must focus on the purpose of your appointment, not ramble all over the map; nor is this the time to perseverate on special topics or interests.

During the interview itself, take notes, whether through writing or taping. Many people don't feel comfortable being taped, so you must get their permission when you set up an interview time if you plan to tape them. If you are going to write notes, practice ahead of time. Only write the essentials; most of the time you want to be looking at the person, not at your notepad.

One of the most important pieces of information to come from an interview are the names of others to interview, as well as ideas and resources for your job search. Make sure you get the person's correct spelling and job title, if there is one; that is very important for a professional job search.

Finally, when it is time to go, thank the person again and shake his or her hand. Go over your notes as soon after the interview as you can. Highlight the most important information and add it to any kind of database you are keeping. Finally, be sure to send a short thank-you letter within a week of the interview.

Gathering background information. The other important way to learn about your community is by reading the local newspaper, business publications and any professional publications for the fields you are exploring. Make notes about businesses that look interesting, trends that would affect your job search.

For instance, you are really good at budgeting and tracking income and expenses, so you decide to go into bookkeeping. However, you find out that one trend affecting small businesses—your target market—is the wealth of do-it-yourself financial software programs on the market. That trend means that small business owners could do their own bookkeeping, resulting in less business for you. By keeping up with these trends, or changes, you will be able to protect yourself better in our global marketplace by changing the focus of your services.

Although this sounds like a lot of work, the process of finding the livelihood that is right for you can be pretty enjoyable. You get to meet new people, expand your horizons, and learn about your community in the process. You will become an expert on careers in your particular area, community or town and may one day get to pass on that information to others.

Know Your Industry

The final step in locating a career or job for yourself involves learning about the field in which you want to work. In other words, after practicing informal interviewing to discover what kinds of jobs are out there, you are now narrowing your search, zooming in on specific jobs. This is where informational interviewing comes in.

Informational Interviewing

Through informational interviewing, you are able to find out about different employers and, sometimes, they are able to find out about you—without the stress of a real job interview. Once again, though, you are not to ask for a job during the interview; instead, you are to simply ask the interviewee about what he or she does on the job and about the trade or profession.

How do you get started? The following list will help get you going.

By treating this as a research project, your career search will be less stressful and more effective. Informational inter- viewing can be a low-stress, enjoyable venture that ultimately teaches you a lot about the job search process and about yourself as well.

Table 5.8: Steps in Setting up and Conducting
Informational Interviews

1. Go back to the list of people and organizations you compiled in the informal inter- viewing stage and make a list of the people to whom you would most like to speak. Add to that list the names of people and organizations about which you have read in the newspaper as you did your community research. Write these individuals a letter, explaining your purpose and then make a follow-up telephone call to set up an appointment.

2. When you set up the time, make sure you tell the person you are not looking for a job with his or her organization but merely want to learn more. Then, make sure you never, never ask for a job during the interview.

3. Practice your interviewing technique with people you know before you head out for your first interview. Once you are ready for a "real" interview, go to people you know the best on your list or to people in a field that is less appealing to you. This will give you good, risk-free practice.

4. Prepare questions ahead of time and take them to the interview. Ask concrete questions, starting with the most basic one, "tell me what you do."

5. Although making small talk is not something individuals on the autism spectrum do well, it is necessary to start off the interview with relaxed

conversation in order to build rapport with the interviewee. For example, ask how the person is, and then remind him or her why you are there and that you are not looking for a job from them at this time. Never go into sensitive topics. Relax as much as possible, for that will also make your interviewee relax. The interview will go better that way. Think of the interview as simply a "conversation" between interested individuals, for that is what it actually is.

6. Always, always leave at the agreed-upon time—unless your interviewee wants to extend the time. When you do leave, make sure you thank the individual in person, leave a business card, if appropriate. Also send a thank-you note within a week of the appointment.

7. Keep notes of your interviews, summarizing the information, including personal information that might be useful later on. Create a chart of information—potential employers, contacts, address/phone and referral source—by "area of interest" (see Table 5.9).

Table 5.9: Summary of Informational Interview

Name: _____

Position: _____

Company/Organization: _____

Referral Source: _____

Address: _____

Phone/e-mail: _____

Date	Type of Contact	Comments	Follow-up

Referrals, suggestions: _____
_____
_____

Resume sent: _____ Date: _____

Thank-you sent: _____ Date: _____

Adapted by permission from J. Benjamin, B. Stanny, & K. Duffy. (1995).
How to Be Happily Employed in Kansas City. *Kansas City, Missouri:*
Career Management Press, p. 30.

Conclusion

Finding a job need not be the dreadful experience that many conjure it up to be. Think of it as a way to not only become employed, but to learn about your community and become a meaningful part of it. To find a job that "suits" you, try these steps:

- **Know yourself**—Take some time to discover what you do best in life, reflect on how to turn your talents into paying jobs. Write about your discoveries and observations in a journal or record your thoughts about them into a tape recorder.
- **Know your community**—Who do you know that could help you navigate the job market? Make a list of family friends, church, temple, synagogue members, neighbors, teachers—all the people you know—and start talking with them about their jobs. What do they like and what don't they like about their work? Keep good notes.
- **Know your industry**—Read about your field, interview people working in the field to find out about the ups and downs of the job. When you have gathered all this information, make sure you write your "30-second commercial" to use in job interviews.

It's important to know what jobs are good matches for you, and what's out there in your community and industry. The next step is to take that information and explore the field. In Chapter 6, we will cover an important area in your job search, the types of jobs that are best suited for the thinking styles of individuals on the autism spectrum. You'll also be reading about the global economy that affects all of our jobs these days and some ways to keep up with it.

CHAPTER 6

Do What You Do Best

Before you actually land your first job as an adult, there are two very important pieces of information you must have. One has to do with how you "think," the other concerns the economy in which you live. If you can work at a job that matches how your brain processes information, you will be better off in the long run. At the same time, the more you know about the economy, the easier it will be to navigate it. This chapter has information on both those topics.

The Way You Think

Know how you process information. I personally think in pictures, not words. That is, when I hear spoken words,

I immediately, without knowing it, translate them into pictures in my mind. While that may sound odd, I have found that there are many of us—on and off the autism spectrum—who think this way. We are "visual thinkers."

For instance, when one of my clients tells me about his concerns about a livestock chute design, I immediately turn those words into a movie in my head, view it and then store it in my "mental file cabinet." Here the information goes into my long-term memory available for me to pull back up when I need it again.

Thankfully, I have excellent long-term memory, the storage unit in the brain. At the same time, I have very bad short-term working memory. For example, if I try to do two or three things at the same time, I will get frazzled. Therefore, for me to be in a job that requires that kind of "multitasking" would be pure disaster. I am not alone. Most people on the spectrum, whether high- or low-functioning, have poor short-term working memory, but often they have better long-term memory than most people.

Autistic brains tend to be specialized. I have noticed they tend to be good at one thing and not so good at something else. In general, there are three different specialized brains: (a) visual thinking, thinking in pictures; (b) music and higher-math brains; and (c) verbal lists and language translator brains (Grandin, 1999). Following are lists of jobs that use the talent of each type. These are jobs that would be careers instead of just jobs. These are also jobs that have a low barrier of entry when compared to medicine and law, for example.

The first group, jobs for visual thinkers, requires little abstract math and hardly any multitasking that relies on the fast information processing that occurs in short-term memory. Instead, they utilize visual thinking and long-term memory, two major strengths for individuals on the spectrum. These jobs would also be good for people with dyslexia. Many dyslexics are visual thinkers, and they also have problems with multitasking.

Table 6.1: Jobs That Would Be a Good Fit for Visual Thinkers

- Architectural and engineering drafter
- Photographer
- Animal trainer
- Graphic artist
- Jewelry maker and other crafts
- Web designer
- Veterinary technician
- Auto mechanic
- Machine maintenance technician
- Computer troubleshooter
- Theater lighting director
- Industrial automation programmer
- Landscape designer
- Biology teacher
- Satellite map analyst
- Plumber
- Heating, ventilation and air conditioning (HVAC) technician
- Photocopier repair technician
- Audio/visual equipment technician
- Welder—There is a huge shortage of people to repair, invent, and building specialized industrial equipment

Table 6.1 *continued*

- Plant engineer
- Radiological technician
- Medical equipment repair technician
- Industrial designer

Music and math minds think in patterns of numbers or musical patterns. Children with this kind of thinking often have a knack for music, and math is easy for them. They tend to be nonvisual thinkers who are good with numbers, facts, and music. See Table 6.2 for sample jobs.

Table 6.2: Jobs That Would Be a Good Fit for Music/Math Brains

- Computer programmer
- Engineer
- Physicist
- Musician/composer
- Statistician
- Math teacher
- Chemist
- Electronics technician
- Music teacher
- Scientific researcher
- Mathematical data mining analyst
- Stock and financial investing analyst
- Actuary
- Electrician

Table 6.3 lists jobs that generally are well suited for nonvisual thinkers who are good with numbers, facts, and foreign languages: in other words, people with more verbal brains. When they were young, they were interested in lists and numbers. An example of a common childhood interest would be memorizing all the baseball batting averages. These jobs also put little demand on short-term working memory but do require excellent long-term memory.

Table 6.3: Jobs That Would Be a Good Fit for Nonvisual Thinkers with More Verbal Brains

- Journalist
- Translator (May be replaced with artificial intelligence)
- Librarian
- Stocks and bonds analyst
- Copy editor (Will probably be replaced with artificial intelligence)
- Accountant
- Budget analyst
- Bookkeeper and record keeper
- Special education teacher
- Speech therapist
- Inventory control specialist
- Legal researcher
- Contract specialist for auto dealership
- Quiet specialized retail sales. There have been some success in selling specialized products such as auto parts, new cars, sporting goods or business

Table 6.3 *continued*

insurance. The autistic person is appreciated for
their knowledge of the products

- Historian
- Technical writer
- Bank teller

The types of jobs that are very bad for people on the autism spectrum are those that require multitasking, doing several things at one time. I would have difficulty doing many entry-level jobs, such as being a cashier, that require making changes while talking to a customer. Taking dictation would be difficult due to auditory processing problems. Also, working as a receptionist would probably be a very bad job for me because so many things would be going on at once. In general, we need jobs that involve doing one task at a time.

Table 6.4: Multitasking Jobs That Are Typically a Bad Fit for Individuals on the Autism Spectrum

- Cashier in busy store
- Waiter in a busy restaurant
- Receptionist who has to both talk and work on the computer
- Nurse in a busy hospital
- Manager in busy organization or business
- Bartender
- Police officer

Table 6.4 *continued*

- Pharmacist in busy drugstore
- Doctor in busy clinic
- Casino worker
- Desk clerk in a busy hotel or car rental agency

A Look at How Artificial Intelligence
Will Affect Employment

If a job is hands-on, it will not get replaced by Artificial Intelligence (AI). Hands-on jobs fixing things will never go away. Live concerts and live theater will still be around. For the visual thinkers (object visualizers), the jobs that are most likely to be eliminated are website programming and animation jobs. For the Music and Math Pattern (visual spatial) thinkers, lower-level computer programming and statisticians may be eliminated. People who work at the highest level of statistics and programming will still be able to make sure the AI computer programming is correct. For the autistic verbal thinkers, the jobs most likely to be eliminated are data entry, translators, copy editors, and book indexes. During the last few years, I have observed that verbal thinkers have been very successful at specialized retail. The person who would be good at their jobs is the one that can memorize many facts. Some real successes have been in selling new cars, sporting goods, and specialized business insurance. I talked to two banks who have autistic individuals successfully selling complex financial products. In all of these jobs, the person is valued for their specialized knowledge of the products. They can help customers find the right product for their needs.

Since the publication of *Developing Talents* in 2008, I found research studies that clearly show that there are visual thinkers who think in photorealistic pictures and there are music and math thinkers who think in patterns. They are two different kinds of thinking. My kind of mind is called an "object visualizer" and the other kind of mind is called a "visual spatial." It is patterns versus photographs. An autistic person is more likely to be an extreme object visualizer or an extreme visual spatial thinker. Many people are mixtures, or they are highly verbal and think in words. To learn more about research about different kinds of thinking, you can read: Grandin (2022). Grandin and Panek (2013), Kozhevnikov et al. (2002), Kozhevnikov et al. (2005), and Perez-Fabello et al. (2016).

Follow Your Interests

When you are thinking about the kind of work you want to do, follow your interests but be practical, too. If you go to college, pick a major that is likely to lead to a job. For example, computer science is generally a good choice. In fact, I am convinced that many of the best programmers have autism or at least some of its traits such as poor social skills and obsessions with a single topic.

Other good majors for individuals on the spectrum include accounting, engineering, library science, and art with an emphasis on commercial art and drafting (to ensure making a living). Generally, majors in history, political science, business, English or pure math should be avoided. It is very difficult to find jobs with just those degrees. However, you could major in library science with a minor in history, as the library science degree would make it easier to get a good job.

If you are the parents of young people on the autism spectrum, please encourage your teenager to take college-level courses in drafting, computer programming, commercial art or other subjects of interest while still in high school. This can help these students stay motivated at a time when life can feel pretty confusing.

Social Skills

You also need to learn or polish some social survival skills—listening, eye contact and conversational skills to start with. The workplace is a social institution, and politeness and grooming count for a lot. There also can be stiff competition for jobs, and the more polished you are, the better you will do. I realize this is not easy for those of us on the autism spectrum, but it's important to at least try. More than likely, you will make friends at work by talking about your shared interests. My social life is almost all work-related. That is, I am friends with people I do interesting work with.

As mentioned earlier, to survive in the workplace, you must learn diplomacy. Even if the boss is acting badly, do not tell him or her so. For that matter, bluntly telling colleagues they are acting badly will not help your cause either. It is important to learn how to tell people negative things without insulting them. Separating the offending behavior from the person is a good first step. Protecting yourself from the problems of coworkers is a second step.

Financial and Other Record Keeping

Other survival skills you must have include learning how to handle your finances and proper record keeping. For instance, when I get a bill, I pay it the day I get it, so I don't forget. For my business, I also had financial experts show me how to create the necessary records to track my income and expenses. I charge flat rates for my services and mark the payments and the job itself on my checkbook stub. That keeps the record keeping easy, and then I am more successful at it.

The 21st-Century Economy

The second piece of information you need before looking seriously for a job or career is what is going on in the economy in general. You need to know this so you can be prepared for the ups and downs of our global economy.

One of the hallmarks of the economy in the 21st century is innovation. Innovations are constantly bringing changes in how we run our business, schools and our lives. The 10 fastest growing occupations require some form of post- secondary education to even step into them.

Knowledge Economy

Basically, the 21st-century economy can be summed in one word: technology. Technology has drastically changed the workplace, from manufacturing plants to school rooms to small offices. It has sparked new life into the American economy and created new types of jobs. There is a huge shortage of high end skilled workers. These people are needed to repair specialized equipment and keep basic services running, such as electricity and water.

You will be living and working in this global economy for the rest of your life, so you must educate yourself about it, beginning in your school days. Read as much as you can in your daily newspapers and national publications such as *The New York Times, Business Week, Newsweek, Time, Fortune, Forbes* and *The Wall Street Journal*. All these publications are all available online.

We live in what's called a "knowledge economy." Information and education are now valued most. Not surprisingly, if you look at the United States Department of Labor's *Occupational Outlook Handbook*, you will find that the fastest growing jobs are all technology-related. Information and communication drive our world now.

The growth industries in the United States are in the "Services" category. Three out of five new jobs come from this category, which includes finance, insurance, real estate, government, transportation, communications and utilities. Most of those new jobs will be in business, health, and social services. You will find the fast-growing technology jobs listed in the "Business Services" category.

Health Care

Health care is a huge and varied field, one of the fastest growing industries in the U.S. economy with a lot of different types of jobs opening up, ranging from physician's assistant to nurse to physical therapist to pharmacist. These are good jobs that pay well, but they are not all good choices for those on the spectrum. Why? Because, depending on the workplace, these jobs can be terribly demanding, requiring a great deal of social interaction with a lot of different people and the ability to do several things at the same time.

If you work as a nurse in a nursing home, or in a doctor's office, or if you work as a physical therapist with the very young or with elderly clients, you'll have a better chance of success in health care. The following are jobs in health care that are particularly well suited for those on the spectrum.

Table 6.5: Jobs in the Expanding Health Care Field That Require Low Levels of Multitasking

- Nurse (nursing home or doctor's office)
- Radiologic technologist
- Lab technician
- Research lab technician
- Computer service technician

Table 6.5 *continued*

- Computer network administrator
- Medical equipment repair technician
- Research pharmacist (pharmaceutical company)
- Hospital pharmacist
- Surgical technologist
- Occupational therapist (for children or the elderly)
- Physical therapist (for children or the elderly)
- Research scientist (neuroscience, medical, cancer, heart and other disease research)

Lifelong Learning

The 20 fastest growing occupations all require some form of postsecondary education to even step into them: wind-turbine service technicians, nurse practitioners, data scientists, statisticians, information security analysts, medical and health services managers, epidemiologists, physician assistants, physical therapy assistants, software developers, occupational therapy assistants, actuaries, computer and information research assistants, operations research analysts, solar photovoltaic installers, home health and personal care aides, taxi drivers, personal care and service workers, veterinary technologists and technicians, and veterinary assistants and laboratory animal caretakers (https://www.bls.gov/ooh/fastest-growing.htm. Education after high school is essential for getting a high-paying job in this 21st century global economy, *Occupational Outlook Handbook* whether it is through a community college, vocational school, university, or job training center. You need to know how to learn and know that you will be learning all your life.

Where we once went to school only in our youth, we now have to be lifelong learners in order to keep up with the changes that are constantly occurring around us. For some, that means getting on-the-job training; others may attend classes or log on to online classes. Whatever the mode, education is a lifelong matter now. You will not only be learning on the job, but in schools and seminars as well. It is simply a fact of life that lifelong learning is with us to stay.

When planning for a career or job, do what you do best.

You want to build from your strengths and work in fields that capitalize on those strengths. If you have strong talents, be sure to make a portfolio of your work. A portfolio, whether in paper or electronic form, is a good tool for your job search. In addition, learn as much as you can about today's global economy to better prepare yourself for working in it. Finally, remember to always, always sell your work, not your personality.

In the final chapter of this book, you will meet individuals from a wide range of jobs and careers especially selected as potentially suitable for individuals on the autism spectrum.

CHAPTER 7

Best Jobs for Individuals on the Autism Spectrum

This chapter presents the stories of individuals working in fields that would be good for many on the spectrum. They have some excellent advice about how to get into those fields and stay there. In addition to first-hand experience, the profiles include career information from the U.S. Department of Labor's *Occupational Outlook Handbook*.

The interviewees were selected because of their experience in the professions or fields chosen as good fits for many on the autism spectrum. They were interviewed in different ways: by telephone, in person and by e-mail. Sometimes all three methods were used for one profile.

Meet People on the Job and Learn From Their Experiences

In the best of all possible worlds, a kindly family member would take you by the hand and teach you about the many different kinds of jobs that are out there. In fact, a family member may have done that very thing with you. However, the world of work is a broad and complex place, so it is beneficial to have as many helping hands as possible.

Think of this next section as just that—a series of helping hands that belong to some very talented people who are taking the time to share what they know about careers in their field or industry. Use their experience and know-how to learn more about these professions that range from aircraft engineer to veterinarian assistant. The world of work is a broad and complex place, so it is beneficial to have as many helping hands as possible.

While you're reading, pay close attention to the following:

In the Introduction, notice the background information about the career. This came from the very helpful U.S. Department of Labor's *Occupational Outlook Handbook*. Salary range and growth rate are listed, but the handbook has far more information, both on its web page (www.bls. gov/oco/) and in the book form found in just about every public library in the country. You can get a lot more information from that source.

- Next, read the Insider Advice section that details the interviewee's perspective on the changes occurring in the field or career and the skills and abilities you will need to do well in that occupation.

- Then you will want to study the Breaking In section, which details the kind of education or experience you need to even step into a job in that field.
- In Success on the Job, you'll find advice on how to get promoted in that field, and what employers look for in their staff members.
- The Resources section details the trade publications and associations for that field as well as similar professions.

At the end of the book, in the Appendix, is a list of additional career resources, books and organizations that will make your job search more fruitful. Happy reading!

(Note: Although a number of the professionals interviewed in 2008 for this next chapter no longer work in their fields, their advice is still spot on. However, the employment data has been updated.)

 Profession: Aircraft Mechanic
Azlan Hazeman

Introduction

As a young boy, Azlan Hazeman loved to ask a lot of "why and how" questions. Why was the sky blue? How did the fan's blades keep from falling off? Why does electricity power the appliances? That curiosity—and persistence, his mother would probably add—led him into a perfect occupation for such an inquisitive mind: aircraft maintenance engineer.

For the past 10 years, Hazeman has been relying on this native inquisitiveness and mechanical ability to find and fix problems with the huge aircraft parked in his airline employer's hangar.

"It is my responsibility to ensure that aircraft are serviceable and airworthy before they are being released to service," Hazeman says. "To be more specific, when an aircraft enters a hangar check after flying a certain number of flying hours, my job is to rectify any defects reported by the pilots and carry out scheduled maintenance inspection checks and operational tests as stipulated by the manufacturer's maintenance schedule."

This can include the repair, replacement, overhaul, inspection and testing of the aircraft's electrical and instrumentation, engine and aircraft system. As an aircraft maintenance engineer, Hazeman supervises a team of mechanics, whose work he must certify before the aircraft can be flight ready.

The median yearly earnings for mechanics and technicians was $70,740 in 2022. The 2022 *Occupational Outlook Handbook* reports that the aircraft mechanic field should be healthy over the next 10 years, growing 4 percent, as fast as average for all occupations.

This is a good time to explore aviation jobs, as the industry, concerned about maintaining a stable supply of pilots and mechanics, has increased wages, and opened additional flight schools. The Federal Aviation Administration is also supporting these workforce development efforts including awarding grants to youth interested in aviation.

Insider Advice

The most sought-after jobs are with large airlines, which offer higher pay and travel benefits. You need some pretty strong work experience, though, to be eligible for those positions, and a track record of keeping up with the technological changes in the field. Further, the competition for those jobs should heat up as airlines continue to consolidate and adopt automated inventory control systems.

According to Hazeman, "In general, there are not many trends that directly affect this field apart from our aircraft maintenance practices and the performance of our parent company. If the business is running well, we'll be very busy with maintenance. If the world economy is not good, as happened during the SARS epidemic, for example, some of our aircraft will be grounded, leaving us in standby mode."

To do well in this field, first, understand the theory behind the aircraft system very well and, second, have adequate experience fixing various defects and troubleshooting problems. The more you have worked on normal and abnormal aircraft defects, the faster you will be able to fix them. If you come to the airline with a lot of experience and a deep understanding of aircraft systems, you'll spend less time checking the manual. You'll save the airline a lot of time and money because aircraft will be able to depart on time.

"A successful engineer is one who can carry out necessary tasks and rectify defects on time," Hazeman says, "plus manage the mechanics working under him or her."

Breaking In

In high school, get a strong background in mathematics, physics and English in order to understand aircraft theory. The rest will be taught during the four years of training, which includes on-the-job and in-class training. Physical fitness and health are also necessary to be able to work the three rotating (day, evening and night) shifts and to be able to handle the physical rigors that go along with the job. You do a lot of climbing and walking as an aircraft mechanic or engineer.

Success on the Job

To be promoted in this field depends on seniority and experience with many types of aircraft. Normally, promotions include becoming lead engineer, supervisor, or superintendent. In general, these positions are over the entire aircraft maintenance crew (engineers, mechanics and apprentices) to ensure that teamwork and cross-functional responsibilities are being handled satisfactorily. It is compulsory, of course, to read inspection notices or aircraft manufacturers' bulletins of current issues, so that you can keep up-to-date on any problems with existing aircraft and the development of new aircraft.

Resources

For more information about this field, contact:
Professional Aviation Maintenance Association
(https://www.pama.org/)

If aircraft mechanic jobs appeal to you, you may also be
interested in other mechanical jobs such as:

- Auto mechanic
- Heating and air conditioning installation
- Electrician
- Copier repair
- Industrial equipment maintenance

 Profession: Artist

Bernadette Torres

Introduction

The "artist" entry in the *Occupational Outlook Handbook*
is wide and varied. It includes jobs such as "art director"
and "animator, "each with its own set of information and
data. This section will discuss "fine and craft artists." To
do this work, you not only have to be talented but also
passionate about what you do to make a go of it.

Or as ceramist Bernadette Torres says: "You have to
do your art every day!" More than half of the artists in the
United States are self-employed, according to the *Occupational Outlook Handbook*. Ask any self-employed person
what it takes to be successful, and you'll hear over and
over: passion, drive and organization!

Besides being self-employed, artists also work for organizations as teachers, art directors, animators, multimedia artists, illustrators, painting restorers and a host of other jobs. With technology such a huge part of our world, artists are also putting their talents to work creating special effects, animation and other visual images for video, film, computers and other electronic media. In other words, artists do it all!

Employment for artists between 2022-2032 is expected to grow by 4 percent, as fast as the average for all occupations, reports the *Occupational Outlook Handbook*. The median salary range for fine and craft artists is $53,140 but is higher for those working in particular industries. For instance, federal government and motion picture artists' median annual earnings is around $100,000. Special effects artists and animators, an art-related job particularly attractive to those on the spectrum, make a median annual earnings of $98,950.

Self-employed artists' earnings vary, depending on their experience and art form. Many artists have other jobs and operate their freelance art business as a sideline.

Insider Advice

Bernadette Torres has been making art since she was a small girl in St. Petersburg, Florida. Her "working career" began in the fourth grade. When her family could not afford the tuition for her art program at an after-school youth center, the teacher "hired" her as a teacher's assistant.

"I even won Volunteer of the Month for my work," Torres laughs. "The mayor gave me a plaque."

Torres is a ceramist who is also on the art faculty at a college. She went into teaching after holding a number of different kinds of jobs. "I missed working with students a lot," she says.

She attributes her drive to be an artist to a number of excellent teachers who encouraged her throughout her school years. With her instructors' help, Torres learned to always do her best work and to be professional. That is something she advises all budding artists to do as well.

Breaking In

Training and education vary by art specialty, but, in general, some formal postsecondary education is necessary to work as a fine artist. Many colleges offer a bachelor's degree in fine arts programs as well as master's degrees. These programs focus more on studio work but having a solid grounding in core subjects such as English, math, social science and the natural sciences is also important.

Torres found that although her college prepared her well for her work as an artist, it did not do so well in training her for a "career" in art. When she wanted to go to graduate school, she found she had a difficult time writing the necessary letters and essays.

"I may have had a difficult time with writing, but I knew who to turn to for help," she says. "I wrote what I needed to say, and then went to friends who were in journalism and other fields to help me refine it."

Art schools are doing a better job now of teaching general education subjects to their students, Torres says. To teach fine arts on the college level, you must have a master's degree. For elementary and secondary schools, a teaching certificate and bachelor's degree are necessary. Other art jobs such as illustrators and art directors have their own educational routes, so be sure to check the Department of Labor's the *Occupational Outlook Handbook* for that information.

For many art jobs, you will need to build a portfolio.

Always, always document your artwork with photographs, Torres advises. She also suggests young artists try everything, learn how to do a variety of different art forms and jobs. Once desperately needing a new job, Torres took the advice of a friend who said, "Become a costume designer; all you do is glue on sequins."

So she went to the Yellow Pages, found seven costume design firms and sent off photographs of costumes she had designed for herself over the years to the firms. Within days, she had an interview and was hired as a costume designer—even though she didn't know how to sew, a big part of the job. "I learned to sew on the job," Torres says.

Success on the Job

First of all, Torres advises, be professional. And always, always ask for what you want. Learn how to talk with people, even if you are shy. That talking will help you find opportunities within your field as well as build connections with people who are interested in your work.

Keep doing your art every day, even if you have a day job that doesn't involve art. Be visible with your work and apply for grants, fellowships, scholarships, competitions, everything. It will help promote your work as well as provide additional revenue.

Finally, Torres advises, know your business, whether that is the freelance art business, design industry, or animation field. Know it inside and out, for it will help you do well and love your work even more.

Resources

For information about art and design, check out:

The National Association of Schools of Art and Design (https://nasad.arts-accredit.org/)

If being an artist appeals to you, you might like art talent jobs such as:

- Architectural or engineering, drafting and design
- Graphic design
- Jewelry making
- Web page design
- Commercial art for advertisement

 Profession: College Professor

Stephen Shore (The following is unique in that Stephen Shore is a person on the autism spectrum.)

Introduction

Today, most jobs that provide a living wage require some form of career-connected postsecondary education. This category includes a variety of teaching positions, ranging from those that require a PhD, such as a four-year university or college, to vocational-technical positions in institutes and schools that specialize in training students for specific careers, one of the main reasons students attend college and university. The best job prospects for postsecondary teachers are likely to be in rapidly growing fields such as health specialties, nursing, business, and education.

The median annual earnings for all postsecondary teachers were $80,840 in 2022. The four highest paid categories were law, economics, engineering, and health specialties, with median annual earnings above $100,000.

Keep in mind that higher education budgets are determined by their state legislatures, and that many of the teaching jobs in postsecondary education are part-time. That trend is not expected to change in the near future.

Insider Advice

Like many other professors, Stephen Shore's career encompasses much more than his teaching duties at a college in Boston, where he is on the music faculty. Shore, who is on the autism spectrum, does consulting and writing in addition to making presentations about autism. Echoing the trends mentioned above, the biggest changes Shore has seen in his teaching career is that the student body is becoming increasingly diverse in terms of age, culture, and nationality. In addition, Shore points out, more and more students with disabilities of all types are enrolling in postsecondary institutions. As a result, educators must learn more than ever before how to teach to the students' strengths.

"We are in the business of education, so we have to broaden our repertoire of teaching methodologies and assessment," Shore says. "We have to get away from 'downloading' data into students' heads and having them regurgitate."

Good teachers must be more like facilitators, Shore says. Other necessary strengths and skills include being able to:

- Organize and present information in a variety of ways in order to teach to students' various learning strengths.
- Make a connection with students, determining their skill and ability levels, and creating a class curriculum with those in mind.
- Teach on multiple skill levels, for classrooms are full of students with varying strengths, back- grounds, and abilities.
- Use a variety of technology in the classroom, including computers, and software programs as teaching aids.
- Keep abreast of one's field and incorporate new research and information into teaching.
- Serve on academic and administrative committees.
- Advise and counsel students about their degree programs and career choices.

- Supervise graduate students' teaching and research and conduct one's own research projects, if in a four-year institution.

Breaking In

To teach for a community college's general education programs, you need at least a master's degree in your field.

Vocational teachers often just have an undergraduate degree and experience in their field, whereas university faculty members must have a doctoral degree. Generally, four-year universities and colleges stress research more than the "art of teaching," so if you are interested in working with students, the two-year community colleges may be your best bet. Many instructors learn the business of teaching by working at it part time, which is also an excellent way of knowing if it is the right field for you.

Become technology-savvy, if you are not already, for many institutions are relying on distance-learning strategies such as online and television courses to reach their far-flung students—as well as to expand their markets.

Often promotions in the field of education mean a move out of the classroom and into administrative positions. Think this move through carefully, for those positions are often very different from classroom instruction and require different skills and abilities.

Stephen Shore advises finding a mentor at your college to help guide you through the minefield of college politics. You don't even have to tell the mentor you are on the autism spectrum if you don't want to but build a friendship with someone you trust who will take an interest in your career and work.

One of the drawbacks of teaching for those on the autism spectrum is being able to recognize your students' faces, Shore says. "It can take a long while to get to know your students," he admits. Shore's strategies to cope with this issue include taking class roll every day and being honest with students about his problems with learning their names. Another tool would be to have students create name tents that include illustrations of their career and personal goals—in color! Then have students introduce themselves, using the name tents.

Resources

Definitely read *The Chronicle of Higher Education* and the *Community Colleges Journal*, both good sources of information, as is the Association of American Colleges and Universities (www.aacu-edu.org).

For information on adult and vocational education, contact:

Association for Career and Technical Education (https://www.acteonline.org/)

If teaching appeals to you, other jobs that require teaching include:

- Coaching a sports team (especially in a specialized sport)
- Teaching karate, yoga or other physical activity
- Teaching in a vocational or technical school where

you teach a technical subject at which you are really good

- Teaching in a special education program

 ## Profession: Computer Programmer

Pat Brown

Introduction

Computer technology has changed the way we run our businesses, our schools, and even our personal lives. The people who write the instructions that drive, test, and maintain software languages are computer programmers. In addition to creating the instructions, programmers also develop ways for computers to solve problems.

Programming is very much a niche occupation. That is, creating instructions for the financial services industry is very different from writing instructions for state governments to monitor school districts' progress, for example.

Compared to other computer technology jobs, such as network systems analysts and computer software applications engineers, programming is declining, decreasing by 11 percent between 2022 and 2032, according to the 2022 *Occupational Outlook Handbook*.

In 2022, computer programmers held about 147,400 jobs and earned a median salary of $97,800.

Pat Brown has been a programmer for more than 20 years with an electrical utility. She has watched programming become far more sophisticated and computers able to solve ever more complex problems. One of the far-reaching changes she has observed was the dot-com bust.

"Programming just isn't as freewheeling as it used to be," Brown notes. "People don't move around as much anymore. I don't know this for sure, but college degrees may have become more important to employers."

Insider Advice

In recent years, industry has become more interested in standardized computer programs rather than creating brand new ones. As a result, more attention is being focused on configuring existing systems, Brown points out.

Breaking In

When asked how you break into the programming field, Brown advises, "This has been true forever, but don't worry about where you start, just go ahead and start. There's a good chance you'll be moving elsewhere and the technology will change in three years anyway, so get experience. Experience counts more in this field than most."

People get into programming with two-year associate's degrees, bachelor's degrees, or vocational training under their belts. Rarely, Brown says, do you see someone with a master's degree. With technology changing so quickly, such a degree may not be helpful.

Success on the Job

Strategies vary in this field by the specific industry in which you are using your computer skills but, in general, promotions do not happen in the way they do in other fields. People often step out on their own, starting their own programming and consulting businesses. One of the reasons for such entrepreneurship is that companies' need for programmers ebbs and flows, depending on their work load.

Programming is also one of those jobs that can be done long distance. Witness the number of American companies shifting their programming jobs overseas.

Keep up with the changes in programming languages as well as the changes in your particular niche. Be flexible and learn all you can to stay up-to-date with this fast moving field.

Resources

Read *PC World* and *InfoWorld* for general programming information, Brown advises, but more important, keep up with your particular industry or niche by reading related trade or professional journals.

Check out these trade and professional associations as well as those in your particular industry:

The Institute of Electrical and Electronics Engineers (https://www.ieee.org/)

Association for Computing Machinery (https://www. acm.org/)

If you are interested in computer programming, it may be best to choose jobs that are not likely to be outsourced to overseas offices. Some of them are:

- Computer network administrator for a large company
- Freelance computer specialist who solves computer problems with both hardware and software (people in these roles visit offices to fix computer problems and set up new systems)
- Computer programmer for a medium-sized business that is too specialized to outsource work to people overseas
- Computer security systems consultant

 Profession: Drafting

(This profile is a bit different from the others, for it involves two individuals with whom I've worked quite closely over the years, Rick Jordan and Mark Deesing. Because this is my field, I've included a few of my own comments.)

Rick Jordan
Mark Deesing

Introduction

As a livestock facilities designer, I rely on drafters to take my designs and translate them onto paper. The designs have to be exact in order to work, and they have to be well drawn, whether by computer or by hand.

Two of the best drafters I know are Rick Jordan, who works for a large meat packing corporation, and Mark Deesing, who works with me at Grandin Livestock Handling Systems. Both learned to draft by hand, which, in my opinion, is the absolutely best way to get started in this field.

Many companies use computer-aided drafting (CAD) programs, but often the most complex designs have to be drawn out by hand.

Drafters work for many types of organizations, all the way from architectural and aeronautical firms to oil refineries and electronic firms. Their job is to prepare the technical and specific drawings and plans for buildings, pipelines, industrial machinery, refrigerators, toys, and anything else that is manufactured or constructed. To do so, drafters use drawings, sketches and codes that instruct production or manufacturing crews in how to build the products.

Drafters held about 197,300 jobs in 2022, with 49 percent working for architectural and engineering firms. Another 23 percent of drafters work for manufacturing firms. This field is expected to decline by 2 percent between 2022 and 2032, partly due to increased use of CAD systems that allow architects and engineers to perform tasks once done by drafters. Median annual earnings for drafters were $60,400 in 2022, with those working in construction and architectural/engineering firms earning the most.

Insider Advice

Rick Jordan works as the head corporate projects designer for a large corporation specializing in the meat industry. In drafting the designs for the company's facilities and machinery, Rick acts a liaison between engineers and production crews. Rick studied drafting at a vocational college, completing the course in just one year. After he finished the program, he assisted the instructor as a student teacher of sorts and actually considered going to college to become an instructor himself.

"However, a large Colorado meat packer required a mechanical drafter and my instructor made me go for an interview to get experience in job-seeking skills. I was hired immediately after my interviewers saw my hand-drawn section of a valve," Rick admits.

Rick is not entirely sure what has helped him be successful, but he does know that as a visual thinker, he creates images as he sees them in his mind's eye—a pretty good trait for a drafter.

"I guess the key to my success has been the ability to teach myself new things and work alone," Rick says. "I have a very understanding and cooperative supervisor and the resources to research new ideas or avenues of progression, both personally and businesswise."

Mark Deesing, another drafter, has worked in the field for six years, all of that time drafting plans for livestock facilities around the world. He is excited about his work, for he has observed over the years that the meat packing industry is growing increasingly more interested in the kind of humane packing plants for which he drafts the plans.

Technology plays a large role in Mark's work. Mark uses auto-CAD and frequently e-mails designs to clients. "I can send drawings by e-mail and a lot of clients don't even require me to visit," Mark says. "I still visit some, though."

For Mark, who used to work as a farrier, shoeing horses, drafting is a wonderful opportunity to use his native creativity. Both Mark and Rick have worked on construction sites, supervising building of their designs. This in-field experience enables them to design projects that work. They also work closely with the end users of their designs to get feedback on how well the facilities worked. Feedback from people who actually use the equipment enables them to continually improve their designs.

Breaking In

For the kind of drafting he does, Mark advises spending time around animals. This is a job that benefits from such hands-on experience. Engineering skills, even if not an engineering degree, are a plus. An animal science degree would also be helpful.

Just as Rick Jordan graduated from a vocational drafting program, you should too. Technical institutes, community colleges, and some four-year colleges offer these programs, says the *Occupational Outlook Handbook*.

In high school, be sure to take math, science, computer technology, and design or computer graphics courses.

Of course, you need to develop a mechanical ability and the ability to draw three-dimensional objects as well as freehand. Finally, be sure to have some understanding of construction and manufacturing standards as well as solid problem-solving and interpersonal skills.

Both Rick and Mark learned to draw by hand before they started working with a computer. This is one reason why their drawings are so good. A person has to learn to draw before learning the computer. Trying to learn to draw at the same time you are learning the computer program is very difficult. I have received drawings from many large companies. The best drawings come from drafters who learned to draw by hand first. These drawings are more detailed and contain fewer mistakes.

Success on the Job

The American Design Drafting Association (ADDA) provides a certification program. Drafters become certified after passing the Drafter Certification Test given periodically at different sites around the country. In addition, employers want to promote those who have the strongest technical and mechanical skills. This means that you must keep up with the changes and advances in technology, as CAD allows for more versatility and range in designs.

Because drafters tend to work for industries that are cyclical, layoffs can happen more easily in this field. This means you have to do your best work and constantly improve your skills. A number of drafters work for temporary staffing agencies and may continue to work through difficult economic times.

"Don't forget," Rick Jordan says, "that the secret to success at work lies in the individual's personal pride and achievement."

Resources

Mark suggests that drafters in his field read industry publications such as *Drovers, Feedlot Magazine,* and the more academic publications *Journal of Animal Science* and *Applied Animal Behavior Science.* In addition, industry groups such as American Cattleman Association and American Association of Agricultural Consultants can provide helpful information for the livestock facilities drafting field.

Whatever field you are in, you must read your industry's trade magazines.

For general information about drafting, check out:

The American Design Drafting Association (https://www.adda.org/)

Some of the places that need good design drafters include:

- Architects
- Large industrial plants of all types
- Building contractors of all types
- State highway departments
- City planning departments
- Engineering firms

Profession: Engineering
Sara Miller
(This profile is a bit different from others, for it involves an individual on the spectrum, who, in addition to discussing her industry, tells the story of her own career path. Sara Miller was diagnosed with pervasive developmental disorder not otherwise specified (PDD-NOS) in 1992, before the term "Asperger Syndrome" was used in the United States. She operates her industrial/manufacturing computer programming business in Minneapolis. This is her story of her career journey.)

Introduction
The development of my career was done more by others—they saw skills and recommended ways of using them. I tried the suggestions and usually succeeded, probably because of my phenomenal literal memory. For as long as I can remember, I have been "mimicking others," or doing what is expected of me by others. Until recently, I never really thought about what it was that I—me—Sara—really wanted to do. That said, here's the progression.

In my junior year of high school (East High School, Green Bay, Wisconsin, 1970-71), the most respected science teacher recommended that I participate in a National Science Foundation summer school program. I attended the program in biochemistry, an intensive six-week

163

residential program in Windsor, Connecticut. I remember it was great being around 49 other smart kids from across the country. We had a group research project, which I continued when I returned for my senior year. I won the Green Bay science fair that year, possibly because some of the judges couldn't even pronounce the title of my project, "Degradation of a Heteropolysaccharide." My sponsoring teacher was proud, but also disappointed that I didn't enter in state, regional or national contests. I didn't see the connection between goofy science fairs—where you had to talk to new and strange people—and scholarships, schools, and future careers. Nevertheless, the experience left me with the feeling, "Well, I could always do something in the science field ..."

I started college at the University of Minnesota because my parents had gone there. Things did not work out, however, probably because I was having trouble meeting new people. Midyear I decided to transfer to University of Wisconsin-Madison, where many of my friends were going. In the meantime, at the suggestion of a girl down the hall in the dorm, I took a class called Nutrition for Non-Majors. I had a blast in that class because I knew most of the content already. My mother was trained as a physical therapist and brought us up with a strong health consciousness. I said to myself, "I can get a major in this? What a piece of cake!" So, upon transferring, I declared Nutrition & Food Science as my major.

After graduation (Dec. 1975) I went to work in the food industry. Everyone thought it was a great field to enter, since everybody has to eat, even in bad economic times.

My ability to handle a significant amount of data and my obsession for exactness led me into the quality control (QC) area of the production facilities. Not a bad place for an OCD/autistic! However, I became very upset when others wouldn't "follow the rules," and would end up quitting and finding another food industry/QC job, until I became disenchanted with the next group of people.

In the late 70s and early 80s, computers were being installed into food manufacturing machines. Again, because of my logic/binary skills combined with a great memory, I was assigned to help develop the specifications for automating various processes. Then I was assigned to learn how to program the special industrial computers. Another piece of cake for me!

After running circles around my boss and his peers, I again was disenchanted with the intellectual level. With my lack of social skills and sometimes strange responses or behavior, I didn't know how embarrassing I was to these people. In my mind, all I was doing was stating facts. Corporate loved me and wanted to promote me.

The locals wanted me fired. So I quit ... again.

Since I had been introduced to the industrial programming field and most people thought I was an engineer anyway, I decided to return to school to work on a Computer Engineering Technology associate degree from Milwaukee School of Engineering (MSOE). The first years of engineering classes follow a certain technical sequence. Since I already had a degree, I didn't need to take any of the general studies courses. So, I filled up my time teaching Quality Control & Statistics courses for MSOE in the Continuing Education Department. I also started to freelance my already developing programming skills as an independent contractor.

After the course of study was completed, I did not pursue a formal job with an established company. The independent contractor situation suited me just fine—I could focus on the details of solving customers' problems and, when done, I could get the heck out of there, thus avoiding any involvement with political games and silly chitchat with coworkers.

It was during this phase that I was diagnosed with PDD–NOS. I also met Temple that first year, and we were amazed at how similar the structures of our businesses were. We both worked as single persons operating a business out of our homes.

Insider Advice

Except I wasn't smart enough to leave well enough alone.

My father was a successful entrepreneur and my mother saw to it that her five daughters were trained in the manners and etiquette of being presentable in public. Those skills, along with that good memory again, led others to suggest that I should start another company designed for a small group of industrial contractors or consultants who shared administrative assistance. In January 1995, NOVA Systems Inc., an industrial systems integration firm, was started.

The ups and downs of small company ownership now entered my life. It was much more emotionally difficult than I had anticipated, and I was not prepared. The typical people skills of independent contractors don't lend themselves to teamwork. So, in summary, I'm happy if my "career" is considered to be an industrial/manufacturing programmer. I'm not so happy with—and definitely would not recommend for people with ASD—ownership of a business that has several employees.

Industrial automation or systems integration is my field.

Over the last two decades, as the price for hardware has come down, there are more opportunities for acceptable return on investment for retrofitting older machines with the newer electrical controls. However, in down economic times, machines are allowed to limp along with their old methods, and business can be slow. We are now entering an upswing, which will help the industry as a whole.

Another fact affecting the industry is overseas competition. With the continued development of the capabilities over the Internet, U.S. integrators/programmers have to be really good and sell on their proximity for quick service. The good news is that many high-level members of the autistic spectrum are very good at this type of activity.

Breaking In
As a programmer, learn something else besides programming. Programming is just logic. Programming is only

"translating" human stuff into a set of binary bits (a language) that a machine understands. If you learn French, but never go to France, how do you expect to know the nuances of culture in your communication? Likewise, in computer programming, your ability to program successfully depends on your understanding of the foundational body of knowledge of the "human" subject. For example, I intimately knew the food-manufacturing systems before I found out that "programming" existed.

As an engineer: To work in industrial automation, you have to be well rounded in mechanical, electrical, and industrial engineering—or at least have really good "friends" on whom you can rely for technical advice.

Success on the Job

Truly, a piece of paper confirming a B.S. in engineering is not needed to be successful, but you'll have a hard time getting past the human resources department at many companies without it. Also, various forms of that piece of paper will help with advancement and salary increases if you want to be in management. Many of the technical details can be taught on the job if you have an understanding of physics, motion and electricity. Industrial products are generally technologically ahead of what is presented in most schools.

The skills and talent that are needed include:

- Logic: ability to organize lots of data
- Detail oriented: ability to see the effects of the small stuff

- Creative: ability to look at things from a different viewpoint
- Quizzical: asking lots of questions to understand the total picture
- Unending desire to learn more: ability to self-teach

Resources

There are gazillions of resources for those in the industry. Here are a few I like:

- *Control Engineering*
- *Manufacturing Automation*

Websites:

- https://automationtechies.com/
- www.manufacturing.net/ctl/
- https://control.com/

Professional Organizations:

American Society for Quality (www.asq.org)

International Society of Automation (www.isa.org)

SME (formerly Society of Manufacturing Engineers) (www.sme.org)

Institute of Electrical and Electronics Engineers (IEEE) (www.ieee.org)

Profession: Financial Accounting & Record Keeping

Sheryl Sunderman

Introduction

If you enjoy working with facts, figures and data, you would do well in the accounting and record keeping fields. Precision and a passion for order are what count in these occupations. For many on the autism spectrum, especially nonvisual thinkers, this kind of work can be very fulfilling.

Basically, the roles of accountants and auditors are to ensure that organizations, companies, and government entities operate efficiently and maintain good records.

Bookkeepers and accounting clerks, on the other hand, do the actual recording of financial data for a wide variety of organizations and businesses. However, the accounting field is broadening to include budget analysis, information technology consulting, and even financial and investment planning.

This means that accountants must come into the field with an even wider scope of abilities and skills. The same advice is good for bookkeepers as well, because the more experience and skills you have, the easier it will be to get hired.

Jobs for accountants and auditors are expected to grow by 4 percent between 2022 and 2032, which is faster than the average for all occupations. The median annual earnings of the 1.5 million wage and salary accountants and auditors were $78,000 in 2022, according to the *Occupational Outlook Handbook.*

The number of jobs for bookkeepers and accounting clerks, which requires less education, is expected to decline by 6 percent between 2022 and 2032, reports The *Occupational Outlook Handbook.* With 1.7 million people working in this field in 2022, it is one of the larger occupations in the United States. Most new jobs will come about due to people leaving the field or retirement. Median annual earnings were $45,860 in 2022.

Insider Advice

Sheryl Sunderman, a certified public accountant, advises people interested in accounting to not only master the necessary financial skills but the communicative skills as well.

Clear verbal and written communication is key for doing well in this competitive business. It is also good practice to know as much as possible about information technology because accounting firms often consult with clients about their technological needs. At a minimum, be very good at using Microsoft Word and Excel programs, the workhorses of the office.

Although the stereotype of the lonely accountant, head bent, shoulders slumped, poring over financial documents is still partially true, at least some of the work day, Sunderman points out that accountants must also have good people skills. Accountants spend part of their time in meetings with clients and colleagues, and teamwork skills are essential for a thriving practice as well.

This is a good time for women to enter the field, Sunderman says; indeed, more women are currently enrolled in accounting college programs than men.

Breaking In

Most accounting jobs require at least a bachelor's degree in accounting or a related field. Some employers want their staff members to have a master's degree in accounting or business administration with an emphasis on accounting. All partners in an accounting firm must be licensed by the state in which they work.

Representatives from accounting firms often visit college campuses to recruit and build their ranks. If this is a field that interests you, and for which you seem to have the requisite skills and talents, visit with them and build a relationship early on with the accounting firms in your area.

Accounting is at least a four-year degree program. It's also important to have an internship, a great way to get work experience while building a relationship with area employers. In addition, start taking bookkeeping and accounting classes in high school. That is how Sunderman started in the business, and this helped her shape her career plan early on. You might even work as a bookkeeper or records clerk while working toward your accounting degree. It is a great way to learn about the business in general.

Success on the Job

Sunderman's advice to accountants wishing to be promoted is pretty simple:

Take and pass the certified public accountant exam. To be a candidate for that exam in most states, you must complete 150 college credit hours—30 more than what is necessary for a typical four-year bachelor's degree. That step is very important toward advancing in the field; but it requires discipline and additional time studying.

- Be willing to work overtime.
- Be able to "multitask"—do several things at once.
- Keep up to date on changes in accounting practice and standards.
- Make your deadlines!

As businesses and other organizations become more "accounting savvy," Sunderman says, so must the accountants who serve them. "Try to learn as much as you can," she advises.

The accounting profession is flexible enough to include several different career paths. The four major fields of accounting are as follows:

- Public accountants—perform a broad range of services, including accounting, auditing, tax preparation, and consulting for a wide variety of clients. They may specialize in taxes, compensation and health-care benefits, and even forensic accounting in bankruptcy cases.

- Management accountants—also work for a wide variety of clients but perform executive functions such as budgeting, performance evaluation, and cost-and-asset management. They are usually part of executive teams involved in strategic planning or new product development.
- Government accountants and auditors—ensure that government agencies and organizations doing business with them follow the law in financial reporting and expenditures.
- Internal auditors—verify that organizations have spent their monies in a proper manner and check for waste and fraud.

Resources

Sunderman recommends reading *The Journal of Accountancy* and *The Accounting Journal* and keeping up with any changing state or professional standards for financial reporting.

In addition, there are a number of professional associations for accountants. This includes the following:

Institute of Management Accountants (https://www.imanet.org/)

The Institute of Internal Auditors (https://www.theiia.org/

For more information on bookkeeping and accounting clerk careers, contact:

The American Institute of Professional Bookkeepers (www.aipb.org)

If accounting appeals to you, you may also be interested in other financial jobs such as

- Stocks and bonds analyst
- Government budget analyst
- Government statistician
- Internal Revenue Service agent
- Sales person for specialized financial products. A major bank has several autistic employees who successfully sell financial products

 Profession: Graphic Design
Kim Tappan

Introduction

For those with a strong visual sense and a creative drive, graphic design can be an interesting and fulfilling career. Graphic designers work for a variety of organizations creating print and electronic designs. Using computer software, graphic designers create designs and layout for magazines, newspapers, journals, corporate reports, and other publications. They also create designs for advertising and promotional displays, marketing brochures, company logos, Internet web pages and more.

Employment for graphic designers is expected to grow by 3 percent between 2022 and 2032, at about the same rate as all occupations. In 2022, median pay for designers was $57,990.

175

This is also a career path full of entrepreneurs, such as Kim Tappan, owner of Tappan Design.

Tappan has been working as a graphic designer since graduating with a bachelor's and master's degree in fine arts. "I didn't want to be a starving artist," Tappan laughs, "so I taught art at the college for a while after graduation."

Insider Advice

Later Tappan went to work for a printing company's art department, where she learned as much as she could as fast as she could. That, in fact, is her first piece of advice: Try everything in order to learn the business.

This can-do attitude worked well for Tappan, who, after the company shut down its art department, bought its equipment and opened her own design firm using the very skills she learned at the printing company.

In her nearly 20 years in the field, Tappan has watched graphic designs become more high-tech and complex—as well as more competitive—thanks partly to the increasing number of home computers and software programs.

Tappan does not try to compete with home-based designers; instead, she focuses on larger, more complex design jobs such as book design.

She also has watched the field become more entre- preneurial as more and more graphic designers open up their own firms. They have had plenty of business, Tappan explains, as small specialty advertising and marketing firms have gone to hiring outside designers for projects.

At the same time, larger organizations have downsized or disbanded their in-house design departments, so they too have hired outside designers for projects.

Keeping up with the changes is critical, whether it's new font designs or new pricing standards. Tappan suggests joining the American Institute of Graphic Arts and the Printing United Alliance, two trade associations whose conferences and publications help her keep up with the business. Tappan also attends the yearly HOW Design Live Conference.

If you are going to own a business, Tappan says, you have to be able to sell your work, so networking and good social skills are a must. If they aren't your strengths, make sure you have someone working with you who can handle that part of the business.

Breaking In

Learn, learn, learn as much as you can, Tappan advises. If you are in college, make sure you get an internship. Design theory is good to have, but working experience is the best teacher, so go to work—even if you have to work for free in the beginning. Learn all you can about computer programs, but make sure you have a practiced eye for good design.

"I see a lot of really talented kids coming out of college, but they don't have good design skills," Tappan points out. "You need to have a good eye for layout and design. I benefited from my fine arts background. It's all about design. I would suggest they take fine arts courses to improve their design. They have mastered a lot of techniques like Photoshop, but how it gets laid out on the page is what makes or breaks the design."

Yet, it is still a good idea to have a college degree, whether it's a bachelor's or a two-year associate's degree from a community college. Attending a trade school would be good, too, Tappan adds. But make sure you learn more than just the basics. If you can, get a background in the printing process.

Success on the Job

Being a good designer is one thing, but building relationships is also important for being successful in the graphic arts design field. Even if you are not self-employed, you still have to have good enough social skills to communicate with clients and colleagues. They are entrusting you with their work, and they want to know you can handle the job, so develop your social skills as much as you can so clients and employers will have faith in you. Always try different jobs in a company to make yourself more indispensable.

Resources

The *Occupational Outlook Handbook* advises designers to not only be flexible and open to new ideas, but to be well read and able to react to changing trends. Good problem-solving skills are important, and so is the ability to work independently and to meet deadlines.

- *Print Magazine*
- *Communication Arts*

- HOW Design Interactive
  (https://howdesignlive.com/)

For information about graphic design careers, contact:
American Institute of Graphic Arts (www.aiga.org)

Other occupations that use similar skills as graphic design include:

- Architectural and engineering drafting
- Still photography
- Video photography (film, movies, or TV)

Profession: Heating, Ventilation, Air Conditioning (HVAC)
Don West

Introduction

If you were one of those kids who took the family toaster and radio apart any chance you got, then working in the heating, air conditioning and refrigeration field might be for you. It is a healthy field, expected to grow by 6 percent between 2022 and 2032, faster than average for all occupations.

Job prospects are excellent, especially for those who have completed training from an accredited technical school or a formal apprenticeship.

It is not hard to understand why there is such growth in this occupation. Air conditioning and heating systems are everywhere—homes, schools, office buildings, factories, groceries, clothing stores, and other businesses. As the world has grown "smaller" and more connected, these once luxuries of modern living have spread far and wide, and so has the need for qualified professionals to install, maintain and repair these increasingly more complex systems, which include mechanical, electrical and electronic components. Although trained to do both heating and cooling, technicians often specialize in installation, maintenance or repair of one type of equipment.

In 2022, the 415,800 heating, air conditioning and refrigeration mechanics and installers in the United States earned a median annual salary of $51,390, according to the *Occupational Outlook Handbook*. About 67 percent worked for heating and air conditioning contractors; the rest were employed in a variety of industries, ranging from fuel oil dealers to refrigeration and air-conditioning service and repair shops to schools and federal and local governments. About 8 percent were self-employed, like Don West.

Insider Advice

Don and his son Bryan do it all. They install, maintain, and repair heating and air conditioning systems in homes and businesses. A former railroad engineer, Don left his job with the railroad when that industry started to look shaky and went to school to learn HVAC. He learned it so well that he now teaches the subject as adjunct faculty at a community college.

In recent years, Don says, a major trend in the HVAC industry has been for large corporations to buy and then consolidate many small and medium-sized heating and cooling companies into larger ones. This enables them to set prices, driving some small mom-and-pop operations out of business. At the same time, Don notes, there are not enough qualified technicians working in the field.

Breaking In

Because HVAC systems have become more complex, employers look for applicants with postsecondary or apprenticeship education, through community college or technical school programs. To learn about the industry, be sure to join and attend meetings of various trade organizations. Also visit with owners of small HVAC companies and see if they would be willing to offer an internship. Expect to start at the bottom and show a willingness to progress.

"I've seen too many students graduate from a program think that they should be able to immediately start earning top pay," Don says. "In reality, they are merely ready to start the learning process."

More and more cities are requiring some kind of certification of technicians working in the field. Also, in order to start a business and obtain a business license, one must be certified as a master by a nationally recognized testing organization.

Success on the Job

You get promoted in this business usually by showing an interest in your work and gaining more knowledge by attending seminars and training sessions, Don says.

Having experience with computer technology is also important for this occupation. HVAC technicians are able to diagnose systems' problems from the field, using cellular technology to access the Internet. In addition, computer hardware and software now allow heating and air conditioning equipment to automatically notify the maintenance department when problems arise.

Resources

Several trade organizations provide information about the HVAC industry, including:

Air-Conditioning Contractors of America (ACCA) (www.acca.org)

Refrigeration Service Engineers Society (RSES) (https://rses.org/)

National Association of Plumbing-Heating-Cooling Contractors (PHCC) (https://www.phccweb.org/)

Other jobs that use similar skills include:

- Auto mechanic
- Industrial maintenance staff (repairs factory equipment)
- Electrician
- Plumber

Profession: Information Technology

Monica Johnston

Introduction

Those born with a curious mind and a tinker's nature may want to try a job repairing the equipment that makes our work—and personal lives—easier. Repairing computers and their networks, office machinery, and even automated teller machines could be a great way to find satisfying employment in these changeable times.

Banks cannot operate without automated tellers, grocery stores don't run if their cash register breaks down, and schools and offices would be at a loss without photocopiers. Given our need for these important machines, we are in debt to the people who show up, repair them, and then leave so we can get back to the business of the day.

These jobs are stable, and given the mobility of today's economy, that is a good thing. As long as there are offices, schools, stores, assembly lines, banks, government agencies, and other organizations at work, somebody has to fix the machines and technology when they break. That somebody might as well be you.

In 2022, there were 914,100 computer support specialist positions in America, spread throughout computer design, in education, finance, telecommunications and other industries. This field is expected to grow by 5 percent between 2022 and 2032, faster than average for all occupations, reports the 2022 *Occupational Outlook Handbook*.

183

Insider Advice

Monica Johnston teaches her students how to use computers as well as repair them at her community college in the Midwest. She started graduate school with a different major but ended up switching after an "aha" moment in one of her college courses.

"I took a required Introduction to Information Technology class in graduate school," Johnston recalls. "The instructor was enthusiastic about computers and technology and her excitement was contagious. By the second or third week of class, I changed my degree emphasis and my career plans."

Many of Johnston's students at the community college are changing careers or starting all over, so her own experience is valuable for her students. She emphasizes that the information technology field has changed greatly over the last decade. For example, it is hard to overstate the influence the Internet has had on business and society in general. The ability to connect to customers creates many opportunities for businesses. However, the Internet is not a panacea. Businesses and individuals lost millions of dollars investing in fledgling "dot-com" ventures in the mid- to late 1990s. The businesses that survived the fallout are now trying to regroup and realistically evaluate the opportunities and challenges created by technology.

Breaking In

"My advice is to be flexible," Johnston says, "for technology changes so rapidly. You have to be ready to respond to these changes and adapt to be successful." Second, she adds, you must commit to a lifetime of training and learning to keep up with the changes in technology.

In addition, you need strong analytical and critical thinking skills. Technical education often does not emphasize communication and interpersonal skills, but these are essential to be successful. Professionals are required to obtain industry-recognized certifications, as well as traditional education and training.

In general, a strong foundation in electronics is necessary to repair computers, office machinery, and automated teller machines. Employers want you to be certified as repairers and have training from associate degree programs, the military, vocational schools, or equipment manufacturers, according to the 2022 *Occupational Outlook Handbook*. Several professional and trade organizations offer certification programs for electronic or computer equipment repairers. Being certified means you have passed several tests assessing your repair skills, which makes you more valuable to an employer.

Success on the Job

The opportunity for promotion varies greatly in the computer repair field. The size of the organization often determines the opportunities for advancement, whether technical or management.

Experience and the ability to keep up with technical changes in equipment will help individuals become promoted. Employers often pay for additional training. The more training you get and the more equipment you know how to repair, the better your chances of advancing in this field.

Resources

The 2022 *Occupational Outlook Handbook* website lists these resources for the computer support specialist field:

Association of Support Professionals (https://asponline.com/)

Technology Services Industry Association (https://www.tsia.com/)

Computing Technology Industry Association (www.comptia.org)

Other jobs that use computer skills include:

- Computer network administrator in a large office
- Repair person for ATM bank machines
- Computer troubleshooter
- Computer setup technician who helps people install new software or hardware
- Repair person for computerized inventory systems in large stores
- Telecommunications and telephone network specialist

Profession: Learning Specialist

Denise Zortman

Introduction

Educational services, one of the biggest fields in the United States today, includes learning specialists and tutor positions, two very important jobs in colleges and universities. These individuals work with students of all capabilities in a wide variety of settings. Sometimes the additional assistance offered by a learning specialist can mean the difference between passing and failing for a student.

Look for learning specialists and tutors in college teaching/learning centers, English-as-Second Language programs, counseling centers, special education programs, and government-sponsored programs for first-generation college students.

Insider Advice

Denise Zortman coordinates the learning resources program at a community college in the Midwest.

"The most important trend I have observed is a lack of student preparedness for college," Zortman says. "Colleges today are teaching more students with developmental needs as well as a lot of adults who are returning to school."

Social issues affect this field as well. For example, welfare-to-work legislation has forced many to seek job training and education. If students have not been in school for a while, they often need this kind of special assistance to learn how to be successful in college. Also, students with various kinds of mild disabilities are enrolling in two- and four-year colleges in increasing numbers as legislation in recent years has mandated supports and accommodations making it easier for students with disabilities to successfully attend postsecondary institutions.

Breaking In

The best way to get hired as a learning specialist is to work as a tutor while in college, Zortman advises. It's a great job for a college student, she adds, for research shows that teaching someone also helps the learner master the subject. You must have at least a bachelor's degree to work as a learning specialist, but many have master's degrees. You might also consider completing a tutor certification program that some professional associations offer, such as the College Reading and Learning Association.

Success on the Job

Because you are working with students of varying abilities, you have to be very flexible. For example, at one table, you may be tutoring addition problems and at the next table you're showing a student how to work differential equations. Develop as many learning strategies as you can, Zortman advises, because everyone learns differently.

With the emphasis on clear writing, learning specialists should have strong writing skills, as many students need help in this area. Even if your job is to tutor math, you can often use writing in coaching students on a variety of subjects. The lack of student preparation is not only affecting community colleges but four-year institutions as well. So, Zortman says, those schools are also offering tutoring programs.

Promotion in this field generally means you become an assistant director or director of a learning center. Sometimes you can even end up working as a college instructor. To be really successful in this very important job, you must work with the "whole" student. That is, you need to take into consideration students' learning styles, their personal and emotional lives, etc.

Resources

College Reading and Learning Association, CRLA (https://www.crla.net/)

National Organization for Student Success (https://thenoss.org/)

Other jobs that use similar skills include:

- Special education teacher
- Occupational therapist
- Speech therapist

 Profession: Library Jobs

Gloria Maxwell

Introduction

Libraries are wonderful places to work. They are quiet, but there is always a lot to do. There are books for browsing, magazines for reading, and technology for exploring the world.

In 2022 there were 141,200 people working as librarians and library media specialists, most of them in school and academic libraries, according to the 2022 *Occupational Outlook Handbook.* A smaller number worked in special libraries or as information professionals for companies and other organizations. The median yearly salary was $61,600 for this increasingly diverse profession.

Employment of librarians is expected to grow by 3 percent between 2022 and 2032, about as fast as average for all occupations. And though library patrons increasingly use library digital services, library staff still host a variety of services and activities.

You don't have to be a reference librarian with a master's degree in library science to work in a library. Library technicians do everything from checking out books, to repairing books, inputting information into computer systems, preparing invoices, handling media equipment, and assisting patrons. If you work in a small library, count on doing just about everything; those who work in larger, urban libraries may get to specialize.

In 2022, some 161,500 library technicians and assistants worked in school, academic and public libraries as well as government agencies. A high school diploma is usually necessary for this job, although some technician jobs require a two-year degree or even a bachelor's. And like many other jobs these days, having computer skills is a must. The occupation is expected to decline by 6 percent over the next 10 years, between 2022-2032, as fewer library patrons need help finding information in person and libraries need fewer staff to operate.

Librarians don't just work in libraries these days. You will find them organizing data for companies, creating databases and reference tools, as well as consulting with organizations about their information systems.

Insider Advice

The biggest change librarian Gloria Maxwell has seen in her field can be summed up in one word: technology! "I think when libraries first started adopting technology, we were suspicious of it," Maxwell recalls. "But librarians need to understand the technology or they will be left behind."

That technology has also opened up new, and sometimes raging, debates over freedom of information. For librarians, access to information is extremely important, but offering Internet services in the library has made that access a dilemma at times. "Librarians have always supported freedom of information," Maxwell says. "And when librarians select a book, it is a choice. But the Internet brings in all sorts of information to libraries that have not been selected. Yet, public libraries still don't want to filter information."

One of the important jobs librarians do these days is teach people how to differentiate between good and bad information, reliable from unreliable. Strong communication skills are necessary for this particular library position as well as flexibility. So if you want to be a reference librarian, develop your communication skills for teaching and demonstrating are key parts of a librarian's daily work.

For those who love to count and work more on their own, Maxwell suggests working in the cataloging and indexing departments of a library. If you love detail work, she says, you will love the rule and guidebooks catalogers and indexers use in their work.

The best way to find out if you would like library work is to work in one, Maxwell advises. Work as a library technician, shelve books while you're in high school, or help staff the circulation desk. That way you will know a lot about what you like and dislike about library work early on.

Breaking In

Once you have decided you like it, you'll need to earn a master's degree in library science in order to work as a reference librarian. If you like the sciences, you have a real edge, for there is a shortage of librarians with a science background, she says.

Whatever your interest, unless you have a library science degree from an American Library Association accredited program, you won't get an interview. Maxwell's advice is to earn an undergraduate degree in a field that interests you and then get a master's degree in library science. An undergraduate degree in library science will not get you the job.

Look outside traditional library jobs for employment, including information brokers, private corporations, and consulting firms. Your research, organizational skills and knowledge of computer databases are very much needed by these organizations.

Success on the Job

Experience counts here, for as quiet as they may be, libraries are busy places and need reliable staff members who are versatile and flexible. If you want to work at a four-year college library, Maxwell advises getting a double master's degree to help you specialize in a field of your interest.

If you work at a small library, where many of the job openings are in the library field, you need to be able to handle as many tasks as possible. Most people flock to big-city libraries for jobs, but the jobs for the next few years are in small towns and rural areas. Plan ahead for this by getting as much and as varied experience as you can.

Resources

American Library Association (www.ala.org)

States have their own library membership and professional associations. Maxwell suggests reading the following professional journals:

- American Libraries
- Library Journal
- School Library Journal
- Academic College and Research Libraries (ACRL)

Other jobs that use similar skills are:

- Journalist (I have met many journalists who work for either newspapers or TV who may be on the spectrum. They have developed a reputation for being good in specialized areas such as science, education or politics.)
- Accountant
- Financial specialist
- Government statistician who monitors markets such as grain or steel

 Profession: Printing
Senta Cisneros

Introduction

One of the most varied industries in the nation is commercial printing and publishing. In 2022, 358,777 Americans were working for printing establishments that do everything from putting out newspapers on time, producing wrapping paper, delivering postcards to resorts, trimming memo pads properly, and printing bank checks with correct account numbers.

Although printing is one of the nation's largest manufacturers, most printing businesses are small, employing fewer than 10 people. This is an industry that is geographically widespread, with printing plants located throughout the country.

Because the jobs are so different, there is not one median earnings figure for this field. As for growth in this broad industry, in general, it is declining slightly but certain jobs such as desktop publishing and magazine and journal printing are growing rapidly.

Insider Advice

For client services manager Senta Cisneros, the workday is fast-paced and full of deadlines. She talks with a lot of people and does whatever she needs to get a customer's printing job completed and out the door on time. By its nature, printing can be stressful, with a lot of deadlines. It is very "client-focused," relies heavily on computer technology, and staff members work together as a team. In general, the smaller the shop, Cisneros says, the more jobs staff members are expected to handle.

Breaking In

However, there are also less stressful positions in printing companies. And although they too must meet the always-present deadlines of a print shop, these employees may have less stress on the job because they don't have to work directly with customers. Some of these jobs include:

- Printing press operators—prepare, maintain, and operate the different types of printing presses. Their duties vary depending on the type of printing press
- Photocopy machine operators—operate and maintain the increasingly more complex photocopy machines

- Graphics specialists—use computers to design graphics for customers' printing jobs
- Bindery machine operators—operate the machinery that combines the printed sheets into the customers' orders, whether it is books, magazines, catalogues, folders, packaging or a wide variety of other printed products

Success on the Job

Depending on the job, you may enter this field by getting some vocational training as well as on-the-job training, Cisneros says. In general, you should have a high school degree with good mathematical, verbal and written communication skills. Definitely be computer literate and be willing to learn more about technology as you continue to work for an organization. Attitude is extremely important and so is a strong work ethic. This is a business that requires flexibility and a willingness to pitch in.

Resources

Because of its dependence on technology, the printing business needs people to stay on top of changes. "The more you know, the more valuable you are in this business," Cisneros says. The more you can juggle, the better off you will be. "The most important thing in this business is change, training and attitude," she adds.

For more information on the printing industry, contact one of these organizations:

Printing United Alliance (https://www.printing.org/)
Graphic Communications International Union
(www.gciu.org)

Other jobs with similar requirements include the following:

- Bindery worker
- Graphic designer
- Advertising salesperson

Profession: Biological & Medical Research Scientist

Ron Jenkins

Introduction

Type in the job category "scientist," and the online *Occupational Outlook Handbook* responds with numerous categories, all the way from "biological and medical scientist" to "federal government." Clearly, whatever your interest, there's a scientist somewhere at work researching it.

That's the good news about this profession. You get to spend time working with scientific ideas, problems and questions that fascinate you. That by itself is a piece of luck. The bad news, though, is that, depending on the particular field, the competition for research scientist positions can be intense. So you'll want to spend some time in the library researching the opportunities and then talk with those working in the field itself.

Now, having said that, there's probably no more rewarding—and interesting—work than being able to spend time studying the scientific questions and principles you find fascinating. For this section, we're looking at the broad category of "biological and medical scientists" and the work they do for research institutions. Some 119,000 people worked as medical scientists in 2022 for a variety of colleges and universities, scientific research and development firms, as well as hospitals and pharmaceutical firms. Employment for medical scientists is expected to increase by 10 percent between 2022 and 2032, faster than the average for all occupations. Median annual salary was $99,930 in 2022, according to the 2022 *Occupational Outlook Handbook*.

Biological scientists held 69,400 jobs in 2022 working at colleges and universities and federal, state, and local government agencies. Employment in this area is expected to increase by 5 percent between 2022 and 2032, faster than the average for all occupations.

Salary varies according to the specialty. For instance, in 2022 the median annual earnings for microbiologists were $81,990; for zoologists, $67,430 53,300, and for biochemists and biophysicists, $103,810. Competition for jobs will continue to be keen. There will continue to be demand for biological scientists specializing in botany, zoology, and marine biology, but opportunities will be limited because of the small size of these fields.

Insider Advice

Those holding undergraduate or master's degrees in the biological sciences will have an easier time finding science-related jobs in sales, marketing and management positions due to their content knowledge.

Biochemist Ron Jenkins followed his interest in health and fitness into a research job studying genetically modified grains for the United States Department of Agriculture.

We will let him tell his own story:

"During the late 1970s, people were becoming more health conscious with regard to eating 'natural' foods and also avoiding foods containing additives and preservatives. I read the labels on food products and could not pronounce them. I thought it would be great to understand why these 'chemicals' are being put into foods, and questioned whether they have a deleterious effect on human health. Red dye no. 2 was taken off the market and nitrosamines were considered as high risk for cancer. So I decided to pursue a 'nutritional science' degree from the University of Florida.

Once I obtained my B.S. degree in nutrition, I was working as a county health inspector. While there were challenges and responsibilities in this position, my true desire was to work in the laboratory, trying to understand disease processes. I knew that I would need more education beyond a B.S. in nutrition. Thus, I completed a B.S. in chemistry with the intentions of going on to graduate school to pursue a Ph.D. in biochemistry.

While working as a graduate student and postdoctoral fellow, I used a molecular biology approach to understand human disease processes in such diverse fields as cancer, immunology, toxicology and related disease. I learned a technique called 'polymerase chain reaction' and used it for several of my research projects. The United States Department of Agriculture needed a person with my background to assist in developing methods to detect the presence of genetically modified events in grains, such as corn and oilseeds. This is the type of research that I am doing today."

Careers don't always follow a straight, or even clear-cut, path, so it's important to know how your skills and abilities can be transferred to different job situations. In Jenkins' case, his use of the "polymerase chain reaction"

(PCR) technique in human disease research opened doors for him at the United States Department of Agri-culture because it was interested in using that PCR technique in its work with genetically modified plants (GMOs).

Breaking In

You must have a strong science background, with a gradu-ate degree preferred. You also need to have good computer and communication skills, Jenkins adds.

There are both science and non-science issues that need to be resolved in this industry. You have to be both a good scientist and a good politician. People who go into science must be patient, persistent and goal oriented. It can be one of the most rewarding professions for those who stay focused, work hard and persevere.

Success on the Job

You have to be able to work independently as well as part of a team. If you are interested in working in private industry, you must demonstrate strong business skills and an understanding of regulatory issues. If you will be doing research in far-away places, you must have physical stamina.

Research scientists usually spend time in a postdoctoral job where they are able to obtain valuable laboratory experience. Sometimes those positions can lead to a permanent job.

In terms of promotions, the federal government employs specialists who review each position's potential promotion, Jenkins points out. These positions are advertised and are available at the USAJOBS website. Generally speaking, the higher your degree, the greater your promotion potential.

Resources

People researching GMOs generally belong to one or more of the following organizations:

- Association of Analytical Chemists (AOAC) (www.aoac.org)
- American Oil Chemists Society (AOCS) (www.aocs.org)

- American Association for the Advancement of Science (AAAS) (www.aaas.org)
- American Association of Cereal Chemists (AACC) (www.aaccnet.org)
- International Seed Testing Association (https://www.seedtest.org/)

All of these organizations contain peer-reviewed publications in their journals.

For information on careers in biochemistry or biological sciences, contact:

Federation of American Societies for Experimental Biology (www.faseb.org)

American Institute of Biological Sciences (https://www.aibs.org/)

 Profession: Language Interpreter/ Translator

Gloria Donohue-Little

Introduction

Do you like to pore over maps and read *National Geographic Magazine*? Is memorizing state capitals and city populations one of your favorite pastimes? If you can say yes to those questions, think about becoming a language translator and interpreter.

Our world is opening up, and international travel and business are much more feasible than just 10 years ago. Technology is creating bridges between nations and people that a few years ago had little to do with each other.

As the world's economy grows more global, more international, there is a greater need for people who can translate documents and interpret for meetings and other events. Companies are crossing borders, operating offices and plants in countries across the globe.

The 68,700 or more language translators and interpreters in the United States have the very important job of making sure we all understand each other well enough to make sure a hospital patient who doesn't speak English gets proper care, that contracts between businesses and their multinational vendors are understood by both sides, and that recently arrived immigrants have their paperwork filled out correctly. Although this is a small field, it is a highly important one for our increasingly multinational world.

Insider Advice

Gloria J. Donohue-Little has 40 plus years of experience in this field, including owning her own business. A native of La Pas, Bolivia, Donohue-Little grew up fascinated by all the different languages she heard spoken around her as a child.

Her company translates documents of all sorts into foreign languages as well as into English. The biggest change she has seen in the translation field is the many different ways her clients can now communicate with each other. From express mail to faxes to internet and software programs, communication has changed and adopted many forms over the years.

The speed of these communication forms makes for a more demanding schedule for translators and interpreters.

There's a big difference between being bilingual and being a translator, Donohue-Little points out. "Most of our translators travel to their country once or twice a year to immerse themselves in the culture and stay up-to-date," she explains. "These visits help them develop the cultural nuances that are terribly important to doing a good job of translating."

Breaking In

To get started as a translator/interpreter, first develop a passion for different cultures and languages. Even developing a deep interest in just one language will help you step into this very interesting business. "Become an expert in that language," Donohue-Little says.

Get training from a university or college and be sure to keep up on the changes occurring in the languages you translate or interpret. Language changes and grows with the country or culture, and to be an effective translator, you must move with it.

A master's degree in the language would be helpful, but Donohue-Little also contracts out to a number of retired professionals—scientists, doctors, engineers and lawyers—for their expertise in their particular field as well as their ability with the language.

Success on the Job

Although Donohue-Little employs primarily independent contractors for her translation business, some translators work for companies and organizations. However, the majority are independent contractors with multiple clients. She advises people to become certified and accredited by the American Translators Association as a way to show ability and skills. This field requires great attention to detail and changes in the language and culture.

Resources

American Translators Association (www.atanet.org)

Other jobs that use similar skills:

- Tour guide
- Editor
- Travel magazine writer

 Profession: Veterinary Assistant & Technician
Jane Jeffries

Introduction

I have had a special love of animals all my life. I spent a lot of time around animals as I was growing up, showing horses at 4-H fairs, helping my aunt with her livestock on her ranch. I don't think I am unusual in my love of animals and feel that many of us on the autism spectrum are attuned to their ways. That is why working as a veterinary technician or assistant is such a great job for many of us.

Veterinary assistants provide basic care for the animals being treated in the clinic. In the course of a day, you will find assistants feeding, watering, bathing, and exercising the animals under their care. In addition, they may clean, repair and disinfect cages as well as provide companionship for animals.

Most of the 114,800 people working as veterinary technicians and animal care assistants in 2022 worked for kennels, clinics, animal hospitals, stables and shelters. The median salary was $34,740 in 2022.

Technicians assist veterinarians with medical treatments, including bandaging, teeth cleaning, installing IV catheters and monitoring anesthesia. In the course of their day, technicians may also perform lab tests, prepare vaccines, take blood samples, maintain equipment and a host of other tasks.

Both technicians and animal care assistant jobs are expected to grow by 20 percent, much faster than the average for all occupations between 2022 and 2032.

Insider Advice

Jane Jeffries has a small animal veterinary practice in the Midwest. To do this kind of work, you have to love animals, of course, but you have to appreciate the people who come with them too, Jeffries says. Being curious doesn't hurt either. "Medicine is sort of like detective work," Jeffries points out. "There's always something new and interesting."

Although animal care is fulfilling work, it can be difficult, both emotionally and physically. You need to be able to protect yourself from the emotional ups and downs that can come with treating ill animals. Develop some kind of system for handling the distress of caring for animals that are in pain, or worse, dying.

Breaking In

First, have animals at home while you're young. There's nothing like growing up around a menagerie of different animals to teach you how to take care of them. The experience is invaluable. Work in a veterinary clinic or hospital; you can even volunteer, suggests Jeffries. Get that hands-on experience.

"Be certain of your choice before spending the college time," she says. Once you do know this is your career choice, take the necessary undergraduate requirements in college before signing up for a veterinarian technician program, usually offered at community colleges.

Success on the Job

Promotion in this field depends on the type of employer with whom you work. Animal care workers at kennels and animal shelters may choose to take the American Boarding Kennels Association home-study program to work toward becoming a Certified Kennel Operator. If you work in an animal shelter, you may take training programs and workshops through the Humane Society of the United States, the American Humane Association, and the National Animal Control Association.

Because veterinary clinics and hospitals tend to be smaller organizations, there is often less opportunity for advancement other than working towards becoming an office manager. That comes with experience, education and proven skill on the job.

Resources

Read industry journals such as *Veterinary Forum*, *The American Veterinary Medical Association Journal* and *Compendium for Continuing Education*.

National Association of Veterinary Technicians (https://navta.net/)
American Animal Hospital Association (https://www.aaha.org/)

Other jobs that use similar skills are:

- Physician
- Chiropractor
- Podiatrist
- Research scientist

CHAPTER 8

Entrepreneurship

For people with disabilities, self-employment can be an excellent way to make a living and be a part of the working world. For me, that world has been my savior. Without work of some sort, life would become small and unsatisfying for me—for most of us, I believe. My livestock-equipment design business has not only paid my bills for a number of years, it has also fed my mind through the interesting projects and people that have come into my life because of it. Starting the business went slowly—it took several years for it to become completely self-supporting. Basically, I started by successfully completing one job at a time and satisfying my clients.

I know I am not alone in this, for 9.5 percent of people with disabilities of all types, about 1.8 million, report they are self-employed (https://www.nationaldisabilityinstitute. org/). My own business grew out my lifelong fascination with cattle and my talent for drawing. I put the two together in forming Grandin Livestock Handling Systems

Inc., and I highly recommend you consider something similar. Look at your talents and think about how you could use them to solve a problem, fill a need or jump on an opportunity you see in the world around you. Notice, I said "the world around you." I didn't start my business because I wanted to spend my days drawing; I saw a need in the livestock industry that hadn't been met, the need for a more humane system of slaughtering cattle and producing meat for American consumers. The world has to want your product or service in order for you to be successful in business.

The world has to want your product or service in order for you to be successful in business.

That is what entrepreneurship truly is: paying attention to what's going on in the world around us and responding to a need or opportunity with a business idea.

There are a lot of benefits to being self-employed, especially if you keep your business concept simple and, preferably, home based. Mine is, and this means I can avoid office politics (too confusing for me), a lot of people talking at once around me (too stimulating), and loud, sudden noises (too startling). I can manage my sensory system better in a home office, and the times when I am working away from my office, I know that I'll be returning there eventually, so it's easier to deal with the distractions on the road. If I have more energy at midnight, I can do the complex jobs then and the easier ones when I am less energetic. Also, with lower overhead, I can put what I save on rent right back into my business.

These days, entrepreneurs are the darlings of governments, media, and higher education. The reality of owning a business, though, is less romantic. It takes a lot of thought, planning, and organization to grow a business, even a one-person sole proprietorship. Add disabilities to the mix, and it can be downright difficult.

But not impossible, says Patti Lind, executive director of Iowa-based The Abilities Fund, a national community development organization advancing entrepreneurial opportunities for Americans with disabilities.

People with disabilities already have a track record of self-employment; they are more likely to be self-employed than other Americans without disabilities (9.5 percent vs. 6.1 percent). For the most part, the businesses tend to fall under the microenterprise category, the smallest of small businesses in the United States. That means they have fewer than 10 employees and require less than $35,000 for start-up costs. Overall, these micro businesses represent 77 percent of all U.S. businesses (Joinsourcelink.com) and their owners are most likely to make you a sandwich, dry clean your suits, clean your office, sell you a bouquet of flowers, unclog your drains, care for your children and paint your house. They are everywhere you look and often unseen, with offices in homes and within other businesses.

"For a business start-up, our clients have to have a great business idea that is suited for them, just like anyone else," Lind says. "There has to be a market need and a demand for it. And the owner has to be dedicated to making a business."

A healthy dose of passion helps, too.

"When we (The Abilities Fund) look at the self-employed, we see people who are passionate about what they are doing," Lind says. " I was talking to one recently, a woman who owns a café, and she told me she still loved to cook as much as when she first started out."

Businesses owned by people with disabilities are like everybody else's. They have to have a solid business concept and a market for their services or products. And despite the many barriers to self-employment (the fear of losing state health and other benefits), a growing number of people with disabilities cite self-employment as a goal. They can help from their state Vocational Rehabilitation Services offices as well as from small business development centers that offer classes and other supports.

Those receiving Social Security benefits can tap into its Plan for Achieving Self-Support (PASS) program as a way to finance business start-up and other costs. With PASS, individuals don't lose their benefits as they grow their business; instead, they are able to invest the extra funds into their business as long as they have a well-developed plan, spelling out the following:

- Work goal
- Income or resources being set aside
- List of supplies, equipment, services needed and their costs
- Timeline for reaching the goal

With the PASS plan, the goals must lead to financial independence or reduction of benefits. The plan is meant to help people with disabilities purchase items, services or skills needed to reach their financial goals. Under SSI rules, any income generally reduces the amount of SSI payments—unless there is an approved plan spelling out the work goal or business idea.

Because the plan is so complex, says Tim McElvoy, a PASS coordinator for the Social Security Administration, it's a good idea to have someone with business plan expertise help write it. PASS applicants can be referred to a VR counselor, who could pay for business training through a Microenterprise Development Organization (MDO), Social Security Work Incentives staff member or others.

One of the more innovative PASS plans he has seen was born out of the client's sheer frustration, McElvoy recalls. The client, a young woman, could not think of a particular talent she could develop into a vocation or a business and was about to give up, when the consultant working with her suggested she start a photocopying service. Using her PASS plan, the client bought a photocopier, which she then moved into a business that had contracted with her to manage all of their photocopying—a business within a business.

To be successful in owning a business, The Abilities Fund suggests entrepreneurs need to hone the following traits:

- Creative problem solving
- Ability to adapt
- Grace under fire
- Persistence
- Willingness to ask for help
- Resourcefulness

Persistence was especially important for me. It kept me going when things went badly. A kind manager at the local Swift plant told me during my twenties that "trouble is opportunity in work clothes." He told me to keep persevering.

During the business-planning stage, Lind also suggests thinking through these questions before getting too far in the start-up process:

- What income level is right for me?
- How much business can I do and stay healthy?
- Can I stay in business if my disability is variable?
- How do I incorporate considerations about my disability into my business plan?

First, realize that you will have to become an expert on entrepreneurship before starting your business. To find a small-business class in your area, check with these agencies or organizations:

- The U.S. Small Business Development Centers (www.sba.gov/sbdc/)
- Kauffman Center for Entrepreneurial Leadership (www.entreworld.org)

- Association for Enterprise Opportunity (microenterpriseworks.org)
- SourceLink (joinsourcelink.com)

Do not go into business for yourself until you have had some business training. In that training, you will learn how to research your industry, target your market and your competition, as well as gain knowledge about all the parts of running a business. In addition, you will learn how to develop and understand the financial documents you will need to conduct your business. Entrepreneurship can be a good career path for people on the autism spectrum, but it will only be as successful as the planning and time you put into it. Please take the time to learn all you can and choose your business carefully. Concentrate on a business that is specialized and one that won't be in danger of being outsourced. Below are a few examples.

- Web design for local businesses
- Highly specialized accounting
- Plumber for older houses
- Electrician
- Heating and air conditioning
- Home repairs
- Unique landscaping
- Legal research in a highly specialized area
- Florist
- Specialized equipment design
- Graphic design and commercial art

- Niche-market computer programming in specialized areas where you do not compete with large corporations
- Locksmith and security systems
- Crafts such as jewelry making
- Architectural and engineering design and drafting
- Consulting, for example, developing individualized education programs for students with special needs

One Entrepreneur's Story

Although Sara Miller was the daughter of a small business owner, she did not start out her working life wanting to follow in her father's entrepreneurial footsteps. On the spectrum, Miller had worked as a quality control specialist and industrial computer programmer for various employers before taking her newly earned computer technology engineering degree and setting up shop as an independent contractor out of her home.

The independent contractor situation suited her just fine because she could focus on solving customers' problems and, when done, could walk away, avoiding any involvements with office politics and socializing with coworkers.

Her business was doing well, she had a good social persona (thanks to her mother's insistence on good manners while growing up), and others suggested she start another company designed for a small group of industrial contractors or consultants sharing administrative assistance. So in 1995, Miller started NOVA Systems Inc., an industrial systems integration firm.

Owning a small company has had its definite ups and downs and has been far more emotionally difficult than Miller anticipated. Working as an independent contractor did not prepare her for the teamwork required of her in her new company. She liked her work as an industrial/ manufacturing programmer, but not her role as company owner and she definitely would not recommend that others with ASD own a business with several employees.

If you decide to go to work for yourself, then remember to plan your business so that it fits your life. Don't try to be something you're not. If you need time by yourself, make sure you choose a business that allows for it. Like to travel? Build that into your business plan. Be sure to design your business, so that both you and it can succeed.

Find out more about Sara Miller's career path in Chapter 7.

CHAPTER 9

Advice from Those Who Have Gone Before

Three Individuals with Autism Tell Their Stories

While traveling for my business and to give presentations at autism conferences, I meet people on the autism spectrum who have been successful in their careers. Often these individuals, many 40 and older, want to help others on the spectrum become successful as well. I would like to thank Kathy Crellin, Larry Moody and Walter Tinney for doing just that. Their stories in this chapter are good examples of the many different paths and routes people take in discovering the work that fits them.

Kathy Crellin—Forecasting Demand Analyst

Background
Kathy Crellin was diagnosed with autism when she was in her 50s and already well into her career. Currently, she is

completing a master's degree in manufacturing technology while working full time. Crellin has found help for her organizational and social skills problems in her Asperger's support group and through Joel Smith's website on living with executive function disorder, www.thiswayoflife.org. This is the story of her career path.

First Jobs

My very first job was a summer job detasseling corn when I was in high school. It was hot and hard work, and there wasn't a lot of stimulation, but I tried really hard and worked really hard. I got the job through a teacher friend of my mom's.

Early Mentors

My mom was my mentor when I was young. She worked as a substitute teacher while we were growing up, and she did a good job of teaching me how to get along at school without interfering too much. I would go home for lunch, and if things were going badly at school, I would tell her about it and we would talk. If they were really bad, she would go up to school and talk with the teachers. She knew me pretty well and, thankfully, she wasn't the type of mother who would dwell on just the problems I was having.

Career Paths

I didn't know what I wanted to do when I went away to college. I had problems the first day my parents dropped me off. I was shy and didn't want the stigma of special education, so I wouldn't see a counselor, which was what I needed. I was far from home, and my first time going home was Thanksgiving. I didn't want to go back after the holiday, but my mother said I had to stay for a year. I had no real focus but ended up majoring in music and history.

After I graduated, I worked at a manufacturing plant near my hometown. The manager was one of my mom's former students. My job was on the production line, putting little pieces into circuit boards. I loved it! I was slow but had a lot of determination, so I figured out how to do it. I had more mentors there because other people working on the line would remind me to look up once in a while and smile, so they would know I was okay.

I thought that you couldn't be successful if you didn't leave home, so I decided to go back to college and study accounting, economics and statistics. I took out a loan, lived in a $30-a-month room and only ate one meal a day: a Big Mac, French fries and an orange drink at 3 PM. I earned straight A's, even though I took 20 hours at a time. I finished the program in two years with a 4.0 grade-point average.

One of my professors told me I had a special talent in statistics, but I didn't get any help finding an internship or a job while I was a student. I really needed a mentor at that point.

After graduation, I worked another manufacturing job and stayed with it for five years. One day I got up the gumption to talk to the production manager and ended up with a job in production control. I worked my way from dispatcher to scheduler to master scheduler to forecasting analyst. I now work at another company as an analyst, a job I heard about through word of mouth.

Success/Problems/Solutions at Work

I think what has helped me finally be successful in the workplace is my stubbornness, or persistence, and the manners I learned at an early age. I was the only daughter in my immediate family, and I had lots of women in my life teaching me—two aunts, two grandmas as well as my mother. I also had something to live up to because my grandma went to college, my mom was a teacher, one aunt was a nurse and another a dietitian.

Another thing that has helped is being active in my trade group, APICS, the Association for Operations Management. This organization offers professional development programs and certification programs for different specialties. In addition, I am working on a master's degree in manufacturing technology.

I have found the following books especially helpful and would recommend them to other Aspies: *Executive EQ: Emotional Intelligence in Leadership and Organizations*, by Robert K. Cooper, which emphasizes teamwork and leadership skills; *The 7 Levels of Change: Different Thinking for Different Results*, by Rolf Smith, which helped me understand the different ways people think and why others may not understand my thinking; and *Leading Quietly: An Unorthodox Guide to Doing the Right Thing*, by Joseph L. Badaracco, a discussion of leadership strategies.

Another characteristic I have had to work on but sometimes fail at is not to get myself all tied up into a knot if I know I am right or I get fixated on one right answer and my recommendation isn't taken. In such situations, I need to work at not having a meltdown or letting people see that my anger is building. I need to not get so personally invested in my point of view, as that can blow things out of proportion.

When I interviewed for my present job, there were six people in the room. I was nervous, but the interview went more smoothly because of my work experience and because I was able to get them interested in a subject I was interested in. Even though I did well in the interview and got the job, it took three months before I would talk to anyone at the company.

Over time I have created some rules for myself about dealing with the social aspects of work:

1. In the lunchroom when I'm getting a soda, I make it a point to talk to anyone who is nearby.
2. There are always a lot of rumors in workplaces, and there are people who love to get everyone stirred up. I am miserable in those situations, so I try not to pay attention. I put my head down and just work.
3. I have learned a lot from others in my autism support group and recommend joining one. The group has helped me learn more about myself and the many different social rules I have to navigate in life.

4. I have learned a lot from Joel Smith's website on organizational skills, www.thiswayoflife.org. I suggest checking that out, too.

Career Advice

The position of demand analyst is a good job for someone with Asperger's. If you have production experience, curiosity, a college degree, or a two-year degree and an APICS certification—along with a mentor—you should be able to land this kind of position.

Another interesting job for someone with autism is to work for a medical devices manufacturer. There are a lot of detail, documentation and regulatory requirements that need to be met as well as setting up compliance processes.

One other thing to consider would be how you approach your education. I read an article in *The Minneapolis Star Tribune* about a growing trend for people to get a four-year degree, maybe in math or science or whatever, and then go to a two-year tech school. I am thinking for someone like me, this would have been a good thing, as it would let me relax a little and just work on the degree, get people experience, and then finish my education when I was a little older and experienced.

As far as the technical side of the demand analyst job, be sure to:

1. Pay attention to detail and learn how to put up with the job tasks you don't like.
2. Learn Excel backwards and forwards and take some business classes.

3. Master statistics for they are important in forecasting.

4. Hone your analytical skills and be able to find root causes.

5. Learn about programming and application

6. Be sure to get an internship in college and find a mentor who can help with advice and career planning.

7. Work as part of a team. To be successful in demand analysis and forecasting as a career, I recommend that people also learn as much as they can about teamwork and leadership skills because they are really important in the workplace. Take any kind of college class on team building.

Larry Moody—Retired Registered Professional Engineer

Background

Larry Moody was diagnosed with attention deficit hyperactivity disorder when he was 52 years old. After trying various stimulant medicines, he and his doctor found one that worked fairly well, but not well enough. Two years later, his doctor told Moody rather abruptly that he had autism, a diagnosis confirmed by a psychologist specializing in it. He was also told that there was no treatment or medication for his condition, a particularly distressing piece of news.

It took Moody a year to realize that he had actually developed wonderful coping skills throughout his life, and he decided that he wanted to help others on the autism spectrum learn to live their lives fully. Those coping skills are persistence, use of eye contact, negotiation, self-confidence, self-control and the ability to physically defend himself.

Several years ago, Moody retired from a thriving engineering practice to care for his wife who was then seriously ill. This is the story of his career path.

First Jobs

My first jobs were mowing yards and babysitting when I was 9 or 10. Probably my first real "outside" work was in my dad's store when I was 13. That first summer I worked 40 hours a week, stocking shelves, cleaning bathrooms, cleaning floors—my dad worked my tail off, but it prepared me for the workplace.

Early Mentors

I did not have a mentor when I was young, at least not in the usual sense. My mother and father were my only mentors then. They taught me more skills than most parents teach their children. Among many other things, my father taught me to use hand and power tools and to diagnose and resolve problems in systems of all kinds. He was strict and demanding, but my mother was kind and patient with me. She instilled in me a belief that I could do anything I set my mind on and a conviction to never give up. My mother also taught me how to be self-sufficient, teaching me to cook, sew and clean. I think she was the single most influential individual in my life, my father being second.

The third most influential person came into my life when I was 22. He was a small, modest Vietnamese man with a big heart, whose martial arts class I hung around and watched until one day he invited me to come in. I soon started training with him; he helped me learn self-respect and confidence and how to defend myself from bullies who had plagued me all my life. Since then I have never again been assaulted. Something changed within me. The bullies and thugs out there no longer sense me as an easy target.

Career Path

Throughout my secondary school years, I excelled at almost anything that was "hands on"—wood shop, drafting, physics and chemistry. I was good at subjects requiring visualization skills too, such as geography and geometry. For almost everything else, my performance was inconsistent and my grades average. At some point in high school, though, I knew I wanted to become an engineer. My senior year physics project took third place statewide in the University of Florida Engineers Fair.

My first engineering-related job was as a drafter. I had taken a half-year of drafting in high school and found it interesting, detailed and mostly solitary work. I took the State Civil Service exam for drafting, passed it and was hired. Later my supervisor told me he chose me because I had scored higher on the drafting exam than anyone he had met in the more than 10 years he had been a supervisor. I realize now that it was one of my special interests.

However, with borderline learning difficulties, I didn't understand just how difficult college was going to be. Even though I got discouraged often, and dropped out several times, I always came back. When not in college, I worked in engineering-related jobs: drafter, technician (designer), and as a computer programmer developing software. I never gave up completely, even if it took me 11 years to get my bachelor of science degree in civil engineering. I took one of my courses five times before getting a passing grade. For most of that time, I worked and went to college part time, taking one to three classes at a time.

Retired for the most part now, my engineering specialty was compressible fluid hydraulics, or computerized gas flow simulation modeling. In other words, I designed and taught other engineers how to design the large and complex piping systems for gasses—natural gas, steam, carbon dioxide, air, nitrogen, hydrogen, etc. I enjoyed my work, I was good at it, and clients sought me out.

I worked most of my engineering career in the natural gas industry, first constructing, then designing, then operating and planning gas piping, compression and processing systems. But when I started my engineering career, I had no idea that's what I'd wind up doing. I spent almost eight years in a variety of pre-professional engineering-related jobs, working closely with many different engineers.

Somewhere along the line, I came to realize that the very best of the engineers I worked with had the most field experience and learned by doing.

I was always willing to take on new challenges that offered learning opportunities. We learn more from the difficult problems we solve than from the easy ones. I developed a reputation for finding cost-effective solutions for problems that other engineers couldn't, or wouldn't, handle. I worked for about 17 years in a variety of engineering and related jobs before being thrown into computerized flow simulation modeling as a result of yet another job change.

Success/Problems/Solutions at Work

I am a visual thinker and always build designs in my head before trying them out on paper or computer. I know early on in a project whether it will work, even before the computer gives me precise numeric results. Early in my career, my employer would send me out to clients with another engineer because I could visualize the project and determine its feasibility. My employer knew not to send me by myself because of my awkward social skills. I sometimes would slip into hyper focus when working on a project or problem. I lose track of time and whatever is happening around me. I've been known to sit at my desk productively working for 8 to 10 hours at a time without food, water or a bathroom break, and sometimes without saying a word.

I'm blind in one eye as a result of unsuccessful cataract surgery at about age 2. This is an example of how a problem can turn into a gift. Although my visual world is and always has been two-dimensional, when I look at blueprints or topographical maps, I integrate the information into 3-D almost instantly in my head. I see all maps and drawings not so much as individual colored lines and squiggles on the paper but as systems of related information, almost as a whole.

One of the reasons why I have been successful in my work, I think, is that I have turned a special interest into a job, and then made my job, whatever it was, into my special interest. Although not always by design, I built my career like a pyramid with a broad base that slowly narrowed into a never pre-determined specialty.

I have always been socially awkward. Not much I could do about that other than try, try again. Early in my professional career, my unofficial mentor, a vice president of engineering, offered me some time with a psychologist that visited the company every year for a week. In two separate one-hour sessions, I learned how poor my eye contact was and then how to remedy that situation. On another occasion, he offered me the opportunity to attend a State Bar Association seminar on negotiating. One engineer and about 999 lawyers! The way these and other special opportunities were presented to me, I thought of them as job perks, rewards for doing good technical work. Little did I know it was essential job training that I needed far more than most of my coworkers.

Career Advice

Don't be in too much of a hurry. If you want to become an engineer, find a pre-professional job working with the type of engineer you want to become. Once you are certain that's the career field you want, then go to school to get the degree. Get as much field experience as you can before moving into project design (you'll make fewer and smaller mistakes). If you need to, or want to, go back to college for an advanced degree. Develop a broad base of knowledge in your field, and then specialize. Accept the fact that it will take time to climb the ladder of experience and credibility toward success.

I believe it takes several approaches to become financially successful:

1. Don't be afraid to change jobs or employers.
2. Develop a career that other people don't want to do or cannot do.
3. Become really, really good at your job.
4. Live within your means, for life is far less stressful when you are financially solvent, and then you can focus better on your work.
5. Work smart and work hard.

Not every job or profession requires a diploma. To be successful in my field, or any other for that matter:

1. First and foremost you need to be able and willing to learn. The "able" part was tough on me, but I was always "willing" when I could see the long-term benefit. In most professions, a diploma is needed, but not always for the obvious reasons. Probably fewer than half of all college programs

actually teach you how to do a job ... they teach you background information and theory, and most important, they teach you how to think and how to approach and analyze a problem or task. The details of almost every job are learned on the job. With the right background and preparation, you can learn quickly, and hopefully not make any serious mistakes.

2. Get promoted by being good at your job. Those of us with challenges have to be better at our jobs than our coworkers to make up for our deficits. You have to do more of what you can do. The quality of your work has to be higher. You have to be willing to volunteer to take on some of the tasks that your coworkers shy away from, especially ones that offer a learning experience. Make yourself more valuable to your employer than your coworkers by increasing and broadening your skills. You have to be persistent and determined to succeed.

3. Be a "team" player. By this I mean, you have to recognize your strengths and weaknesses (know your limitations). You have to be willing to leverage your strengths by constantly being available to help your coworkers learn to do their jobs better, improving their skills. And you have to ally yourself with people who can help you with your areas of weakness. These are both active processes, not passive ones.

4. Realize there will be ups and downs, occasional rapid gains and setbacks. You can change jobs. You

can change industries. You can change fields. But you can never give up.

"Walter Tinney" (pseudonym)—Retired Marketing Executive

Background

Both Walter Tinney and his teenage son have been diagnosed with autism, so in this interview Tinney is focused on his own past and present as well as his son's future. Retired from his executive marketing position, Tinney continues to learn as much as he can about the autism spectrum. He points out that many successful people over time appear to have had Asperger traits—Benjamin Franklin, Albert Einstein, John D. Rockefeller, Isaac Newton, Howard Hughes, John Lennon, Stephen Spielberg and Bill Gates.

"What they have in common," Tinney says, "is that they took control of their lives very early on." They set the pace that others followed. They were all very different thinkers who had a profound impact.

This is the story of Tinney's own career path.

First Jobs

As a kid, I did everything—had a paper route, sold all-occasion greeting cards and flower seeds, cut lawns, shoveled snow and sold cheddar cheese door to door. I worked in a restaurant, clearing off tables and even helping the short-order cook. I also was the president of my Junior Achievement club, for which we had to run a mini-business. I learned a lot about selling techniques from all of these jobs. Nobody taught them to me; I learned by doing.

Early Mentors

I didn't really have a mentor when I was young. I was the oldest of six kids, my father was an engineer and he was busy with his career. But I had an aunt who took me to Broadway plays, art museums and the theater, and she opened up the world for me. For four months, though, I did have a wonderful high school math teacher, who helped me learn and understand math and see how smart I actually was. Before that, I had been a mediocre student, and the school guidance counselor had told my mother to put me in vocational classes, as I would not get into a university. My IQ is in the top 2 percentile.

After working with that math teacher, even for just four months (we moved mid-year), my life changed. From that point on, I was transformed and became a top student. I even decided to put myself back a year in high school, so that I could take the subjects I needed to be admitted to college. Mentoring doesn't always have to be over a long period of time; the ripple effect can sometimes open up doors for you. The key is to find someone who believes in you and helps you to believe in yourself.

My family moved to Montreal when I was in high school, and because Quebec students then graduated after what Americans would consider junior year of high school, I was put back another year. This actually worked out well for me because it gave me more time to mature, which is very important for people with Asperger's. Now I was in classes with younger students, whom I was really much closer to in emotional maturity. I became a leader in high school, filling leadership roles on the student council and in sports, which all helped me grow. When I graduated, I received the Student Council Award for the student who had contributed the most to the school that year. Two years prior to this I never would have dreamed that all this could have happened. I did not know that I had autism until only recently.

Career Path

I studied pre-med for two years before deciding I didn't want to be a doctor (lucky I did not listen to that guidance counselor!). I knew that I was good at publicity and sales, so I changed my major to communication arts and took business and economics courses with a minor in philosophy. I decided I would have a career in advertising and marketing, that I would practice an "up and out" philosophy and never have the same job for more than two years. If I weren't moving forward, I would make changes.

Most of my career changes have been because of people asking me to take on new challenges. I became very skilled in helping to turn businesses around because I thought differently and came up with innovative solutions—a quality many people with autism have. I also decided, in advance, that I would never work more than a 20-minute drive from where I lived—I hate wasting time. This was my plan and this is what I did.

Success/Problems/Solutions at Work

To be successful on the job, I think people with autism who have difficulty focusing need a beacon. For me, this quote of George Bernard Shaw, which I have framed over my desk and have read nearly every day for over 38 years, was my beacon:

"People are always blaming their circumstances for what they are. I don't believe in circumstances. The people who get on in this world are the people who get up and look for the circumstances they want, and, if they can't find them, make them."

This quote had a profound effect on me, and I set goals believing failure was not an option for me.

What gave me problems early in my career was my lack of social skills. I would receive superior performance reviews, but my bosses would also tell me that I was too hard on others and wasn't flexible enough. I had a low tolerance for people who couldn't keep up with me, who did not do their jobs properly, and my bosses wanted me to take the time to explain my vision to others. I was task-driven and achieved excellent results. Results, not people, were important to me.

The Xerox Professional Selling Skills program was helpful in addressing that problem. I was in marketing and went into sales for a few years, which is really all about paying attention to people, listening closely to what they have to say, and understanding different personality types. The Xerox training program taught you how to sell to different people with different needs and personality types in an organized, step-by-step process. It used concrete case studies and even had a fact sheet that classified different customers and situations and how to sell to them. While the program was about sales, it also taught me social skills. This gave structure to a lot of "unwritten social rules." It also improved my social life dramatically!

Prior to this, I had learned from a colleague how to read body language (he had been in U.S. Intelligence), another great skill for business. And a boss taught me that nothing was impossible ... everything has a solution. I really lucked out with these folks. None of this was planned.

I know that I'm very good at distilling a lot of information, processing and summarizing it, and then clearly defining problems and solutions to them. We know that people with autism tend to be literal and can find all the things that are wrong. When I see a problem, I instantly want to solve it. The difficulty is that someone else caused the problem(s), and to get to the solutions quickly the culprit(s) are exposed. This is where other executives need to get involved to handle the people issues.

Career Advice

A lot of people with autism have been successful in business, and one of the things they often have in common is that they took control of their lives. Autistic people like to be in control, and they should get on the road to success early on. So they need some momentum early in life, but unfortunately that doesn't always happen. As a result, an enormous amount of potential is lost. If I were CEO of a company today, I would be certain to have someone with autism on my management team, an innovative thinker who gets results and is not out to win a popularity contest every day. This is the person who will tell you things that others will not. Brutal honesty is a common autistic characteristic.

1. Identify what you are good at. Success builds success.
2. Don't limit yourself; especially don't limit the amount of time you spend on your special interest. Use this as a springboard to broaden your scope by introducing closely related topics. The special interest will drive the quest for more knowledge in a wide range of subjects.

   Just think what the world would be like if Bill Gates had been told, "Okay, Bill, you can only spend one-half hour a day on your interest in computers and software." Your special interest is the starting point for focusing on what could turn into a great career, a career that could have a profound impact on your life.
3. Try to use your special interest to become interested in other subjects at school.
4. Be creative. Focus on a series of "small wins" that collectively add up to "big wins."

5. Don't limit yourself because you are scared to try new things. Push yourself a bit. For example: When my son, who is autistic, was in the eighth grade, he went on a three-day school trip to another city, just like all the other students. The school prepared him for this. The reward for this success was letting him start to take public transportation home from school. Then he learned to ride it downtown. Now he knows how to navigate the entire transit system— this builds self-confidence. We are fortunate that we can travel and, as a result, he has now been all over the world. He has reached the point where he could travel on his own anywhere.

6. Don't limit your education or allow others to do that. Often life for people with Asperger Syndrome becomes one of a "self-fulfilling prophecy"—with more emphasis on "cannot" than on "can." In many respects, autism is a very special gift that should be celebrated, and with the right environment it can allow you to flourish in ways that others cannot.

Don't ever feel trapped in a career path. People shouldn't feel like they are locked into a particular path. Your job should be fun and rewarding. If it is not, then find something that is.

In conclusion, the only person who stands in the way of your achieving something is you.

References and Further Reading

Introduction

Center for Disease Control (CDC)(2020) Data on statistic ASD

Clark, R. W. (1971). *Einstein: The life and times.* New York: Thomas Y. Crowell.

Fitzgerald, M., & O'Brien, B. (2007). *Genius genes: How Asperger talents changed the world.* Shawnee Mission, KS: Autism Asperger Publishing Company.

Grandin, T. (2006). *Thinking in pictures and other reports from my life with autism.* New expanded edition. New York: Vintage Press.

Grandin, T. (2022) *Visual Thinking.* Penguin Random House, New York

Grant, V. W. (1968). *Great abnormals.* New York:

Hawthorn. Kevin, G. (1967). *Inspired amateurs.* Freeport, New York: Books for Libraries Press.

Isaacson, W. (2023) *Elon Musk,* Simon and Schuster, New York.

Ledgin, N. (2001). *Asperger's Syndrome and self-esteem.* Arlington, Texas: Future Horizons.

Sacks, O. (1995). Prodigies. *The New Yorker,* Jan. 9, 44-65.

Vance, A. (2015) *Elon Musk,* Penguin Random House, New York.

Autism Research Institute (www.autism.com). Autism Society of America (www.autism-society.org).

Bauman, M. L., & Kemper, T. L. (1994). *The neurology of autism*. Baltimore: John Hopkins University Press.

Cassano, M. F., et al. (2007). Comparative minicolumnar morphometry of three distinguished scientists. *Autism*, 11(6), 557-569.

Center for the Study of Autism (www.autism.org).

Cesaroni, L., & Garber, M. (1991). Exploring the experience of autism through first-hand accounts. *Journal of Autism and Developmental Disorder*, 16, 169-187.

Courchesne, E. et al. (2001). Unusual brain growth patterns in early life in patients with autistic disorder. *Neurology*, 57, 245-254.

Courchesne, E., & Pierce, C. (2005). Brain overgrowth in autism during a critical time in development: Implications for frontal pyramidal neuron and interneuron development and connectivity. *International Journal of Developmental Neuroscience*, 23, 153-170.

Diagnostic and Statistical Manual (DSM) 5th Edition (2022) American Psychiatric Association.

Mayo Foundation for Medical Education and Research (www. mayoclinic.com).

National Institutes of Health (www.nih.gov).

Uddin, L.Q. (2022) Exceptional Abilities in Autism: Theories and Open Questions, *Current Directions in Psychological Science* 31(6):509-517.

Chapter 2

Alert Program (www.alertprogram.com). Autism Research Institute (www.autism.com).

Banker, S. (2003). Personal interview. Children's Therapy Group. Overland Park, Kansas.

Baron-Cohen, S. (2000). Is Asperger Syndrome/high-functioning autism necessarily a disability? *Development and Psychopathology*, 144, 1288-1292.

Baron-Cohen, S. (2020) *The Pattern Seekers*, Basic Books.

Coleman, R. S., Frankel, F., Ritvo, E., & Freeman, B. J. (1976). The effects of fluorescent and incandescent illumination upon repetitive behaviors in autistic children. *Journal of Autism and Developmental Disorders*, 6, 157-162.

Covey, S. (1990). *The seven habits of highly effective people*. New York: Simon Schuster.

Grandin, T. (2006). *Thinking in pictures and other reports from my life with autism*. New expanded edition. New York: Vintage Press.

Hardy, P. M. (1989). National Conference of the Autism Society of America. Seattle, Washington, July 19-22 (personal communication).

Hartman, T. (1994). *Focus your energy: Hunting for success in business with Attention Deficit Disorder*. New York: Pocket Books.

Huggins, J. (1995). *Diagnostic and treatment model for managing SIB, rage and other hyperadrenergic behaviors in autistic/PDD and DD populations*. Aurora, Ontario, Canada: Kerry's Place.

Irlen, H. (1991). *Reading by the colors*. New York: Avery.

McKean, T. A. (1994). *Soon will come the light*. Arlington, Texas: Future Horizons.

Narayan, S., Moyes, B., & Wolff, S. (1990). Family characteristics of autistic children: A further report. *Journal of Autism and Developmental Disorders*, 20, 523-535.

Robertson, C.E. and Baron-Cohen, S. (2017) Sensory perception in autism, Nature Reviews *Neuroscience* 18(11):671-684.

Ratey, J. et al. (1987). Autism: The treatment of aggressive behaviors. *Journal of Clinical Psychopharmacology*, 7, 35-41.

Robison, J.E. (2012) *Be Different*, Crown Publishing, New York.

Williams, D. (1992). *Nobody nowhere and somebody somewhere*. New York: Time Books.

Williams, M. S., & Shellenberger, S. (1996). *How does your engine run? A leader's guide to the alert program for self-regulation*. Albuquerque, New Mexico: Therapy Works.

Williams, Z.J. et al. (2021) A review of decreased sound tolerance in autism, *Neuroscience and Biobehavioral Review*, 121:1-17.

Chapter 3

Autism Society of America (www.autism-society.org). Bureau of Labor Statistics, U.S. Department of Labor.

Occupational Outlook Handbook, 2008-09 Edition, www.bls. gov/oco/.

Chapter 4

Bolles, R. N. (2021). *What color is your parachute? A practical manual for job-hunters and career-changers.* Berkeley, California: Ten Speed Press (Revised).

Kanner, L. (1971). Follow-up study of eleven autistic children originally reported in 1943. *Journal of Autism and Childhood Schizophrenia*, 1, 112-145.

Robison, J. E. (2007). *Look me in the eye: My life with Asperger's.* New York: Crown Publishing.

Sinetar, M. (1987). *Do what you love, the money will follow.* New York: Dell.

Chapter 5

Benjamin, J., Stanny, B., & Duffy, K. (1995). *How to be happily employed in Kansas City.* Kansas City, Missouri: Career Management Press.

Chapter 6

Bureau of Labor Statistics, U.S. Department of Labor. *Occupational Outlook Handbook*, 2023 Edition, www.bls.gov/oco/.

Grandin, T. (1999). *Choosing the right job for people with autism or Asperger's Syndrome*. Center for the Study of Autism. www. autism.org.

Grandin, T. (2022). *Visual thinking: the hidden gifts of people who think in pictures, patterns, and abstractions.* New York: Penguin Random House.

Grandin, T. and Panek, R. (2013). *The autistic brain*. New York: Houghton Mifflin Harcourt.

Kozhevnikov, M. et al. (2002). Revising the visualizer-verbalizer dimensions: evidence for two types of visualizers. *Cognition and Instruction*, 20(1), 47-77.

Kozhevnikov, M. et al. (2005). Spatial versus object visualizers: a new characterization of visual cognitive style. *Memory and Cognition*, 33(4), 710-726.

Perez-Fabello, M.J.A. et al. (2016). Is object imagery central to artistic performance? *Thinking Skills and Creativity*, 21, 67-74.

Chapter 7

Career information for the profiles came from the U.S. Department of Labor's *Occupational Outlook Handbook* web page (www.bls.gov/oco/). This information can also be found in the handbook's paper version in library reference areas.

GAO aviation report can be found online at https://www.gao.gov/products/gao-23-105571

Chapter 8

The Abilities Fund

Appendix

When to Disclose Autism

People who have mild autism and no obvious speech delay should concentrate on selling their talents when they apply for jobs in technical fields such as engineering, computer programming, scientific research or electronics. Technical companies often employ people with undiagnosed autism, and it is likely you will fit in. There is no black-and-white dividing line between "computer nerd" and autism. It is a continuum, a matter of degrees.

If you need to modify your cubicle to eliminate fluorescent lights, you can disclose that fluorescent lights give you a headache and you need a quiet spot because too much noise and commotion interfere with your concentration.

However, if you get a job in the special education field, it may be an advantage to disclose a diagnosis of autism. People in this field are likely to appreciate your insights.

Individuals with high-functioning autism with more severe symptoms may need to disclose their condition to their employers. They need to make it clear what their strengths are and where their weaknesses lie. A busy receptionist job would be difficult due to all the multitasking. When you discuss autism with your employer, emphasize your strengths and the positive contribution you can make with your talents.

When Do You Disclose Your Disability—If Ever?

When do you disclose, if ever, to an employer? There is no one correct answer to that important question. If you do self-disclose, this information must be kept confidential by law. If you have questions about when to disclose, the following website lists some good ideas: www.unbc.ca/disabilities/dismod1.html

Getting into fights with employers about your rights under the Americans with Disabilities Act may cause more problems than it solves. The legal route is the last resort. Getting into a nasty lawsuit with an employer may get you branded as a troublemaker. There are some situations when a lawsuit is justified, such as being fired after the boss lied to her superiors and told them that you failed to do your job even though you had good performance reviews. Just remember, if you choose to fight, even if you win the battle with an employer, others may be reluctant to hire you. You will be forced to choose between the lawsuit or a career.

The U.S. Equal Employment Opportunity Commission

Facts about the Americans with Disabilities Act
Title I of the Americans with Disabilities Act of 1990, which took effect July 26, 1992, prohibits private employers, state and local governments, employment agencies and labor unions from discriminating against qualified

individuals with disabilities in job application procedures, hiring, firing, advancement, compensation, job training, and other terms, conditions and privileges of employment. An individual with a disability is a person who:

- Has a physical or mental impairment that substantially limits one or more major life activities;
- Has a record of such an impairment; or
- Is regarded as having such an impairment.

A qualified employee or applicant with a disability is an individual who, with or without reasonable accommodation, can perform the essential functions of the job in question. Reasonable accommodation may include, but is not limited to:

- Making existing facilities used by employees readily accessible to and usable by persons with disabilities.
- Job restructuring, modifying work schedules, reassignment to a vacant position.
- Acquiring or modifying equipment or devices, adjusting modifying examinations, training materials, or policies, and providing qualified readers or interpreters.

An employer is required to make an accommodation to the known disability of a qualified applicant or employee if it would not impose an "undue hardship" on the operation of the employer's business.

Undue hardship is defined as an action requiring significant difficulty or expense when considered in light of factors such as an employer's size, financial resources and the nature and structure of its operation.

An employer is not required to lower quality or production standards to make an accommodation, nor is an employer obligated to provide personal use items such as glasses or hearing aids.

Medical Examinations & Inquiries

Employers may not ask job applicants about the existence, nature or severity of a disability. Applicants may be asked about their ability to perform specific job functions. A job offer may be conditioned on the results of a medical examination, but only if the examination is required for all entering employees in similar jobs. Medical examinations of employees must be job related and consistent with the employer's business needs.

Drug & Alcohol Abuse

Employees and applicants currently engaging in the illegal use of drugs are not covered by the ADA, when an employer acts on the basis of such use. Tests for illegal drugs are not subject to the ADA's restrictions on medical examinations. Employers may hold illegal drug users and alcoholics to the same performance standards as other employees.

EEOC Enforcement of the ADA

The U.S. Equal Employment Opportunity Commission issued regulations to enforce the provisions of Title I of the ADA on July 26, 1991. The provisions originally took effect on July 26, 1992, and covered employers with 25 or more employees. On July 26, 1994, the threshold dropped to include employers with 15 or more employees.

Job Tips

Keep in mind these job tips when you are searching for a job:

Try to make sure the projects you work on have a well-defined goal or endpoint. For example: design a system to handle 100 cattle per hour with no electric prod, or program a computer to do accurate speech recognition when a person talks fast.

An example of a poor way to assign a person on the spectrum to a project would be to say: "Your job is to build a new cattle handling system" or "Your job is to develop new computer programs." These instructions are too vague.

You will decide how to do the design work or write the program, but the boss needs to be specific about what the facility or program is supposed to do. The desired outcome of the project has to be specific.

Sell your work, not your personality. Whenever possible, make a portfolio of your work to show what you can do. Develop skills in things that other people want.

Try to make sure coworkers, and especially bosses and supervisors, know your social limitations so they don't suddenly throw you into a complex social situation such as seeing important clients. If you feel it would be inappropriate to disclose our autism diagnosis, tell the boss you are a pure "techie" and that you do your best work at your computer and that too much non-technical work makes you nervous and frustrated.

Knowledge is power in the job search process and in the job itself. Remember to share what you know with others and to always ask questions when you do not understand something.

Further Readings on Interventions to Reduce Sensory Problems

Coleman, R. S., Frankel, F., Ritvote E., & Freeman B. (1976). The effect of fluorescent and incandescent illumination on repetitive behavior in autistic children. *Journal of Autism and Developmental Disorder*, 6, 157-162.

Elliot, R. O., Dobbin, A.R., Rose, G. D., & Soper, H. V. (1994). Vigorous aerobic exercise versus general motor training effects on maladaptive and stereo- typic behavior in adults with both autism and mental retardation. *Journal of Autism And Developmental Disorder*, 24, 565-576.

Irlen, H. (1991). *Reading by colors*. New York: Avery.
Knivsberg, A. M., Reichelt, K. L., Hoien, T., & Nodland, M.

(2002). A randomized controlled study of dietary intervention in autistic syndrome. *Nutritional Neuroscience*, 5, 251-261.

Lightstone, A., Lightstone, T., & Wilkins, A. (1999). Both colored overlays and colored lenses can improve reading fluency, but their optimal chromaticities differ. *Ophthalmic Physiology Optometry*, 4, 279-285.

Miller, L. J. (2006). *Sensational kids: Hope and help for children with sensory processing disorder.* New York: G. P. Putnam/ Penguin Group.

Robertson, C.E. and Baron-Cohen, S. (2017) Sensory perception and autism, Nature Reviews *Neuroscience*, 18(11):671-684.

Rosenthal-Malke, A., & Mitchell, S. (1997). Brief report: The effects of exercise on self-stimulating behaviors and positive responding of adolescents with autism. *Journal of Autism and Developmental Disorder*, 27, 193-202.

Stehli, A. (1991). Sound of a miracle. New York: Doubleday. Walters, R. G., & Walters, W. E. (1980). Decreasing self-stimulating behavior with physical exercise in a group of autistic boys. *Journal of Autism and Developmental Disorders*, 10, 379-387.

Wilkins, A. (2002). Colored overlays and their effects on reading speed (a review). *Ophthalmic Physiology Optometry*, 5, 448-454.

William D. (1996). *Autism: An inside out approach.* London: Jessica Kingsley Publishers.

Williams, Z.J. et al (2021) A review of decreased sound tolerance in autism, *Neuroscience and Biobehavioral Reviews* 121:1-17.

Further Readings on the Link between Creativity, Genius, and Abnormality

Andreason, N. C. (1987). Creativity and mental illness prevalence rates in writers and first-degree relatives. *American Journal of Psychiatry*, 144, 1288-1292.

Baren-Cohen, S. (2000). Is Asperger Syndrome/high functioning autism necessarily a disability? *Development and Psychopathology*, 12, 489-500.

Donnelly, J. A., & Altman, R. (1994, June). The autistic savant: Recognizing and serving the gifted student with autism. *Roeper Review*.

Fitzgerald, M., & O'Brien, B. (2007). *Genius genes: How Asperger talents changed the world*. Shawnee Mission, KS: Autism Asperger Publishing Company.

Grandin, T. (2006). *Thinking in pictures and other reports from my life with autism*. New expanded edition. New York: Vintage Press.

Grant, V. W. (1968). *Great abnormals*. New York: Hawthorn.

Ledgin, N. (2001). *Asperger's Syndrome and self-esteem*. Arlington, TX: Future Horizons.

Further Readings on Creativity

Fitzgerald, M., & O'Brien, B. (2007). *Genius genes: How Asperger talents changed the world*. Shawnee Mission, KS: Autism Asperger Publishing Company.

Luria, A. R. (1987). *The mind of the mnemonist.* Cambridge, MA: Harvard University Press.

Morris, B. (2002). Overcoming dyslexia: Fortune examines business leaders and artists who have gone beyond the limitations of dyslexia. [Electronic version] May 13. ww.fortune.com

Persson, C. B. (1987). Possible biological correlations of precocious mathematical reasoning ability. *Trends in Neuroscience,* 10, 17-20.

Silberman, S. (2001, December). Geek Syndrome—autism and its milder cousin Asperger's Syndrome is surging among the children of Silicon Valley: Are math and tech Genes to blame? *Wired,* 174.

Wheelwright, S., & Baron-Cohen, S. (2001). The link between autism and skills such as engineering, maths, physics and computing: A reply to Jarrold and Routh. *Autism,* 2, 223-227.

West, T. G. (1991). *In the mind's eye.* Buffalo, NY: Prometheus Books.

Career Resources

Americans with Disabilities Act information

U.S. Department of Justice ADA Home Page

www.usdoj.gov./crt/ada/adahom1.htm

Autism Society of America: Offers a wealth of information on its web page, including information on each state's vocational rehabilitation offices, an excellent source of assistance for those who need job training and other vocational assistance. www.autism-society.org

Bolles, R. N. (2003). *What color is your parachute? A practical manual for job-hunters and career-changers.* Berkeley, CA: Ten Speed Press.

Bureau of Labor Statistics, U.S. Department of Labor. *Occupational Outlook Handbook*, 2008-09 Edition, www.bls. gov/oco/.

Center for the Study of Autism: Has information by a number of authors on its web page covering a wide variety of issues. Also offers a lot of information about autism itself. www. autism.org

Clausen, J. (2001). *Too lazy to work, too nervous to steal: How to have a great life as a freelance writer.* Cincinnati, OH: Writer's Digest Books.

Community Services for Autistic Children and Adults: Offers a wide range of social, educational and psychological services for those on the autism spectrum.

Operates a supported employment program for its clients, preparing them to enter the workforce.

Located in Rockville, MD, the organization was started in 1979 by concerned parents of adults on the autism spectrum. www.csacc.org

Edwards, P., & Edwards, S. (1999). *The best home businesses for the 21st century* (3rd ed.). New York: Jeremy P. Tarcher/Putnam.

Farr, J. M. (1994). *America's top jobs for college graduates* (3rd ed.). Indianapolis, IN: JIST Works Inc.

Farr, J. M., & Ludden, L. (2003). *300 best jobs without a 4-year degree*. Indianapolis, IN: JIST Works Inc.

Hartman, T. (1994). *Focus your energy: Hunting for success in business with Attention Deficit Disorder*. New York: Pocket Books.

Hausman, C., & Cross, W. (1998). *The complete small business sourcebook*. New York: Times Books.

iCanONLINE: An online community for people with disabilities; this web page has information about employment, money and benefits, issues and rights and a whole host of other categories. www.icanon- line.net

Kestler, D. (Ed.). (2002). *Career information center* (8th ed.). New York: MacMillan Library Reference USA Group.

Meyer, R. (1999). *Asperger Syndrome employment workbook*. London: Jessica Kingsley Publishers.

Morkes, A. (Ed.). (2003). *Encyclopedia of careers and vocational guidance* (12th ed.). Chicago: Ferguson Publishing.

Morkes, A. (Ed.). (2001). *The top 100 fastest growing careers for the 21st century* (3rd ed.). Chicago: Ferguson Publishing Co.

Schaffert, T. (Ed.). (2001). *Exploring tech careers: Real people tell you what you need to know*. Chicago: Ferguson Publishing.

Parker, L. V. (1997). *How to start a home-based writing business* (2nd ed.). Old Saybrook, CT: The Globe Pequot Press.

Shulen, J. (1998). *Home-based business mom: A basic guide to time management and organization for the working woman*. Santa Barbara, CA: Newhoff Publishing.

Sinetar, M. (1987). *Do what you love, the money will follow.* New York: Dell.

Smith, M. D. et al. (1997). *A guide to successful employment for individuals with autism.* Baltimore: Paul Brookes Publishing Co.

Wright, J.W. (2001). *The American almanac of jobs and salaries.* New York: Avon.

Entrepreneurship

For information on entrepreneurship, try these websites. They offer concrete information about starting small businesses:

The U.S. Small Business Development Centers (www.sba. gov/sbdc/)

Kauffman Center for Entrepreneurial Leadership (www. entreworld.org)

Association for Enterprise Opportunity (www. microenterpriseworks.org)

National Association for Community College Entrepreneurship (www.nacce.com)

Small Business Administration (www.sba.gov)

Temple Grandin

Temple Grandin earned her PhD in Animal Science from the University of Illinois and is currently a Distinguished Professor at Colorado State University. Dr. Grandin is one of the most respected individuals with autism in the world. She presents at conferences nationwide, helping thousands of parents and professionals understand how to help individuals with autism and related disorders. She is the author of *Emergence: Labeled Autistic*, *Thinking in Pictures*, *Animals in Translation* (which spent many weeks on *The New York Times* Best-Seller List), *The Autistic Brain*, and *The Loving Push*, co-written with Debra Moore, PhD. One of the most celebrated—and effective—animal advocates on the planet, Temple Grandin has revolutionized animal movement systems and spearheaded reform of the quality of life for the world's agricultural animals. She lives in Fort Collins, Colorado.

Kate Duffy

Kate Duffy has worked as a transition navigator for both high school and college students with disabilities, focusing on competitive integrated employment. As director of Universal Design for Learning (UDL) for a National Science Foundation-funded research grant exploring ways to increase the number of students with disabilities in the STEM fields, she organized a series of workshops that featured college faculty's most effective teaching and learning strategies. A writer by training, Kate received her M.S. in journalism from the University of Kansas, wrote a monthly careers column for *The Kansas City Star* for six years and has written four books about employment, including two about employment for people with disabilities. She is the mother of two autistic sons.

Books by Dr. Temple Grandin